MW01699891

Young & Giroux

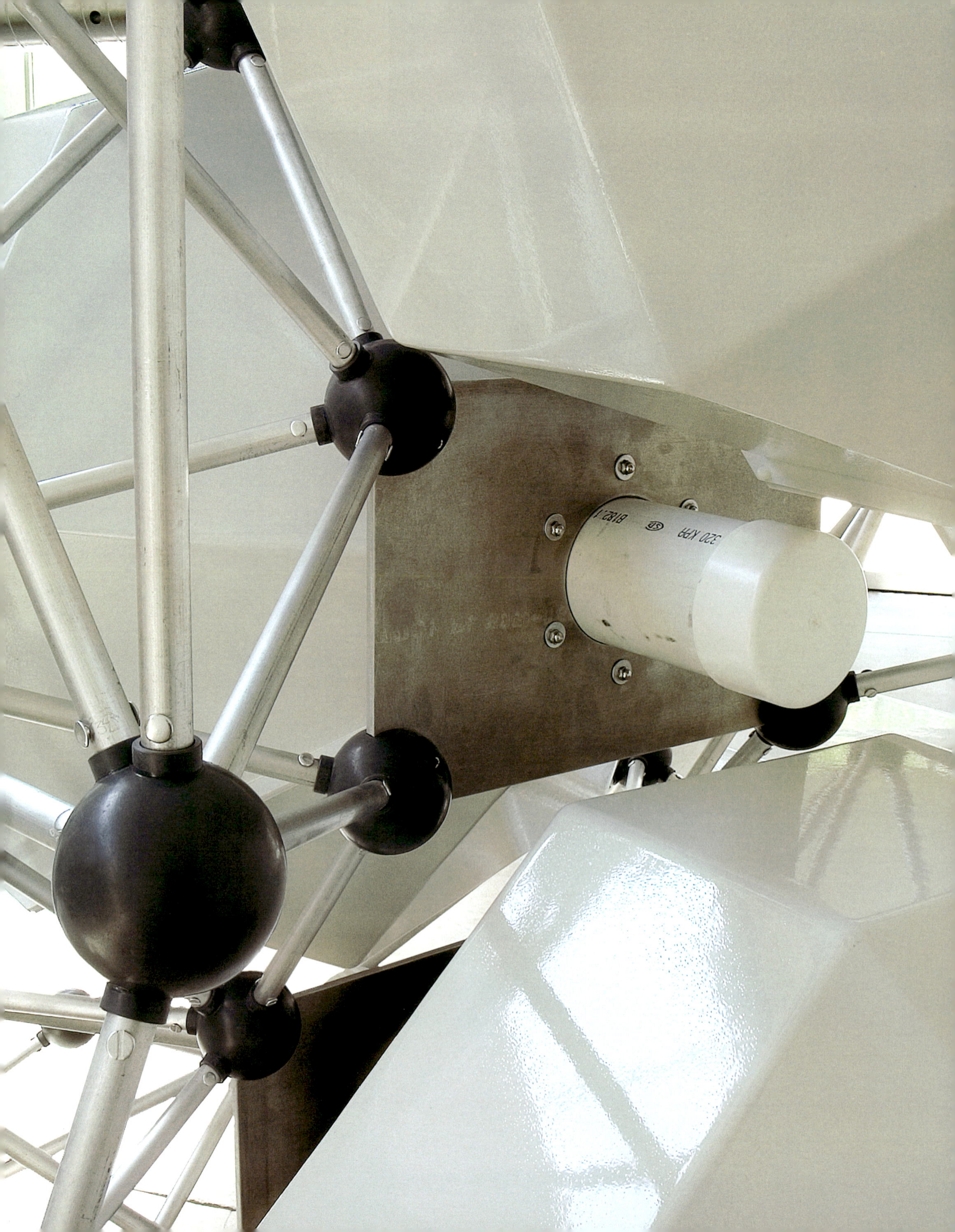

# Young & Giroux

KENNETH HAYES / JESSE HUISKEN / MARK LANCTÔT

Southern Alberta Art Gallery

Library and Archives Canada Cataloguing in Publication

Hayes, Kenneth, 1962-
Young & Giroux / Kenneth Hayes, Jesse Huisken, Mark Lanctôt.

ISBN 978-1-894699-51-8

1. Young, Daniel, 1981-. 2. Giroux, Christian, 1971-. 3. Art, Canadian--21st century.
I. Huisken, Jesse II. Lanctôt, Mark, 1974- III. Giroux, Christian, 1971- IV. Young, Daniel, 1981-
V. Southern Alberta Art Gallery VI. Title. VII. Title: Young and Giroux.

N6545.6.H39 2011 709.7109'0511 C2011-906351-4

Design: Lisa Kiss Design, Toronto
Copy editors: Kathy Daymond, Rosemary Heather, Charlie Huisken, Susan Le Pan
Photography: Rafael Goldchain: pp 29, 33, 35-36, 42; Toni Hafkenscheid: pp 2, 8-11; Galen Kuellmer: p 19;
Guy L'Heureux: pp 63-65; Peter MacCallum: pp 6, 12, 14-15, 25, 40, 45, 47, 49-51, 53-54, 59, 66-69, back cover;
Cheryl O'Brien: pp 23, 37, 39, 70-73, 75; Douglas M. Parker Studio: p 20
Other Images: Images on page 16 from W.H. Mayall's *Machines and Perception in Industrial Design*, 1968.
Permission granted by Design Council/University of Brighton Design Archives. www.brighton.ac.uk/designarchives;
László Moholy-Nagy image on page 7 © The Museum of Modern Art/Licensed by SCALA/Art Resource, NY;
Victor Brauner image on page 7 © CNAC/MNAM/Dist. Réunion des Musées Nationaux / Art Resource, NY;
Digital renderings on pages 31 and 32 by Chris Bahry

Distributed in Canada by ABC Art Books Canada
Printed and bound in Canada by Somerset Graphics

**Publisher**
Southern Alberta Art Gallery
601 - 3rd Avenue South, Lethbridge, Alberta T1J 0H4
www.saag.ca, info@saag.ca

**Page 2:** *IDCSP*, 2006 (detail) **Back cover:** *Kermit*, 2008 (detail)

# CONTENTS



## PROJECTS

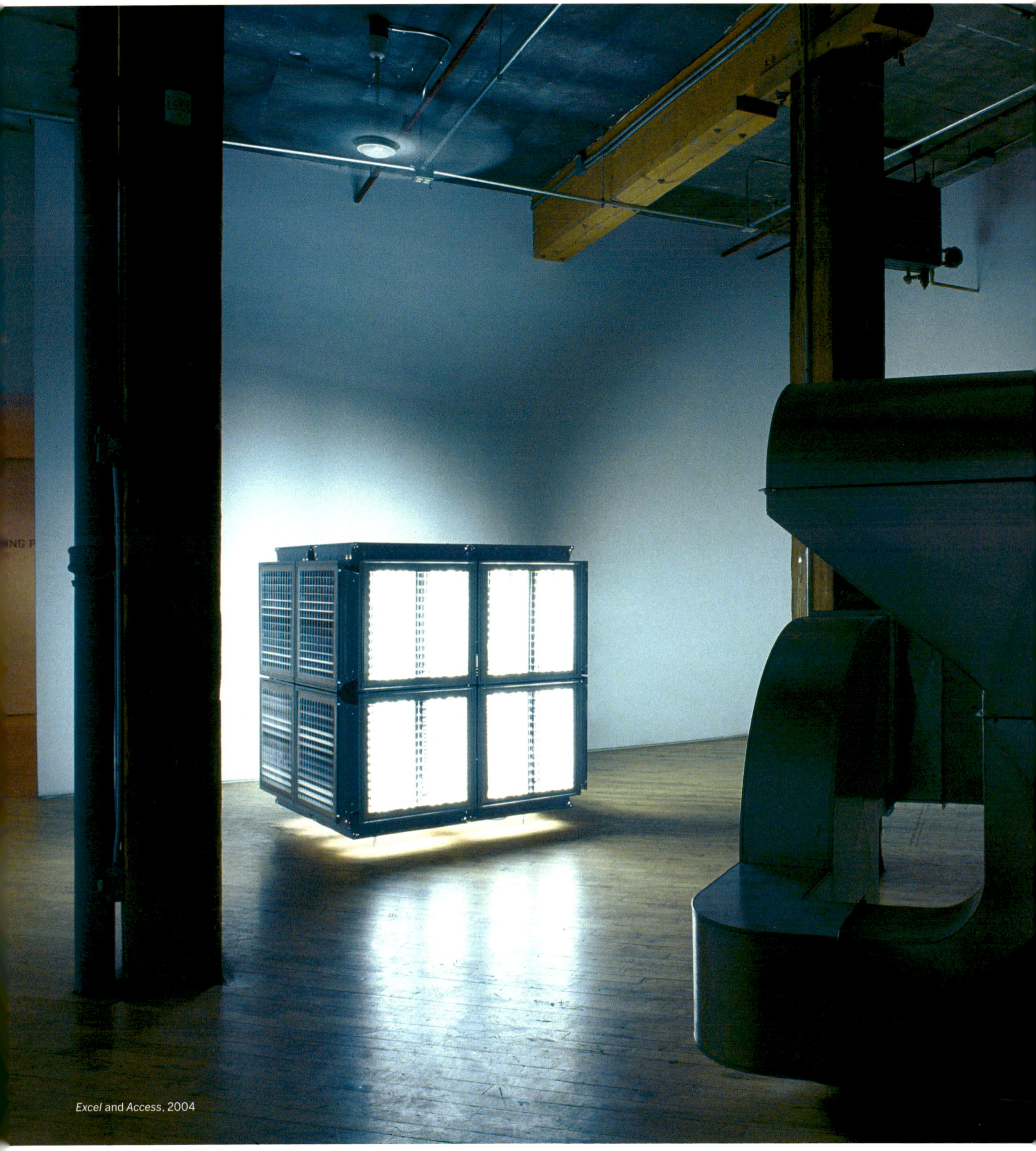

*Excel* and *Access*, 2004

# FOREWORD

We are grateful to Daniel Young and Christian Giroux for their patience and generosity throughout the mounting of their exhibition, *Boole*, at the Southern Alberta Art Gallery and the production of this publication. Lisa Kiss's sensitively designed exhibition catalogue aptly reflects the artists' work while essayists Kenneth Hayes, Jesse Huisken and Mark Lanctôt provide diverse reflections on their practice.

The Southern Alberta Art Gallery is indebted to The Canada Council for the Arts whose commitment to contemporary art production in Canada ensures that gallery audiences have meaningful encounters with a range of current practices. The Alberta Foundation for the Arts, Ontario Arts Council, Cities of Lethbridge and Toronto, Diaz Contemporary, our members, donors and volunteers all contributed to the realization of this project.

**Marilyn Smith, Executive Director**
**Southern Alberta Art Gallery**

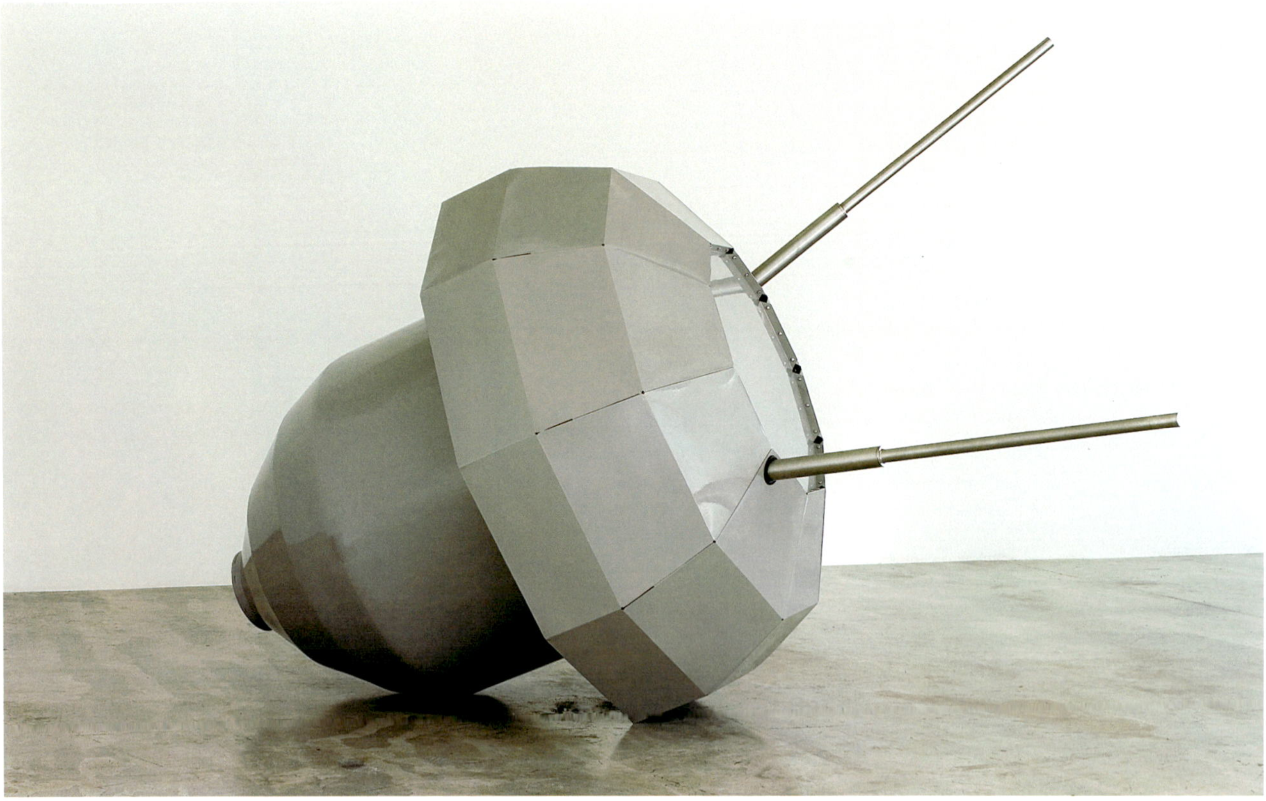

*Cosmos*, 2006
Sheet metal, automotive paint, formed stainless steel tube and fasteners
244 x 152 cm in diameter

*Alouette*, 2006
Powder coated aluminum, machined PVC and fasteners
74 x 81 cm in diameter

**Opposite**

*IDCSP*, 2006
Aluminum tube and plate, PVC, vacuum-formed plastic and fasteners
396 x 244 cm in diameter

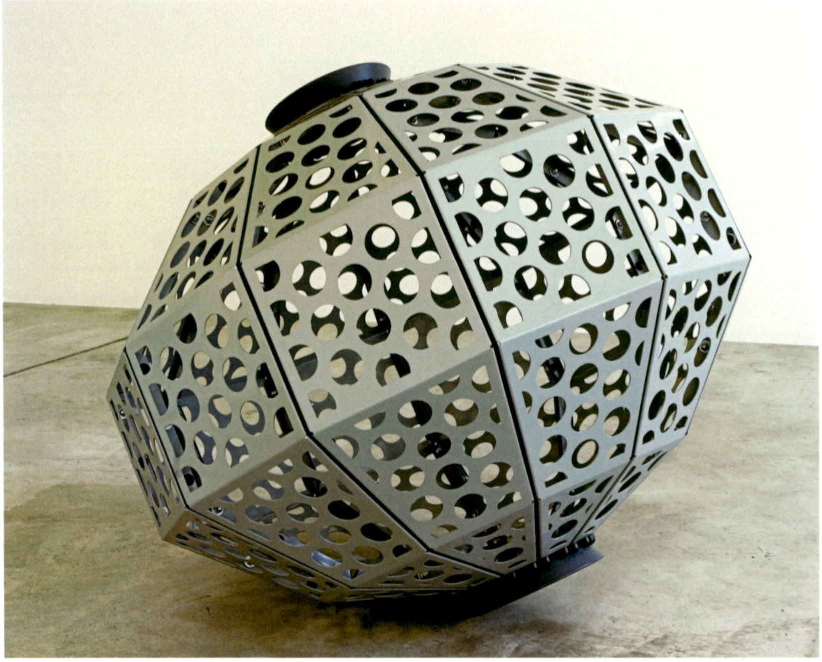

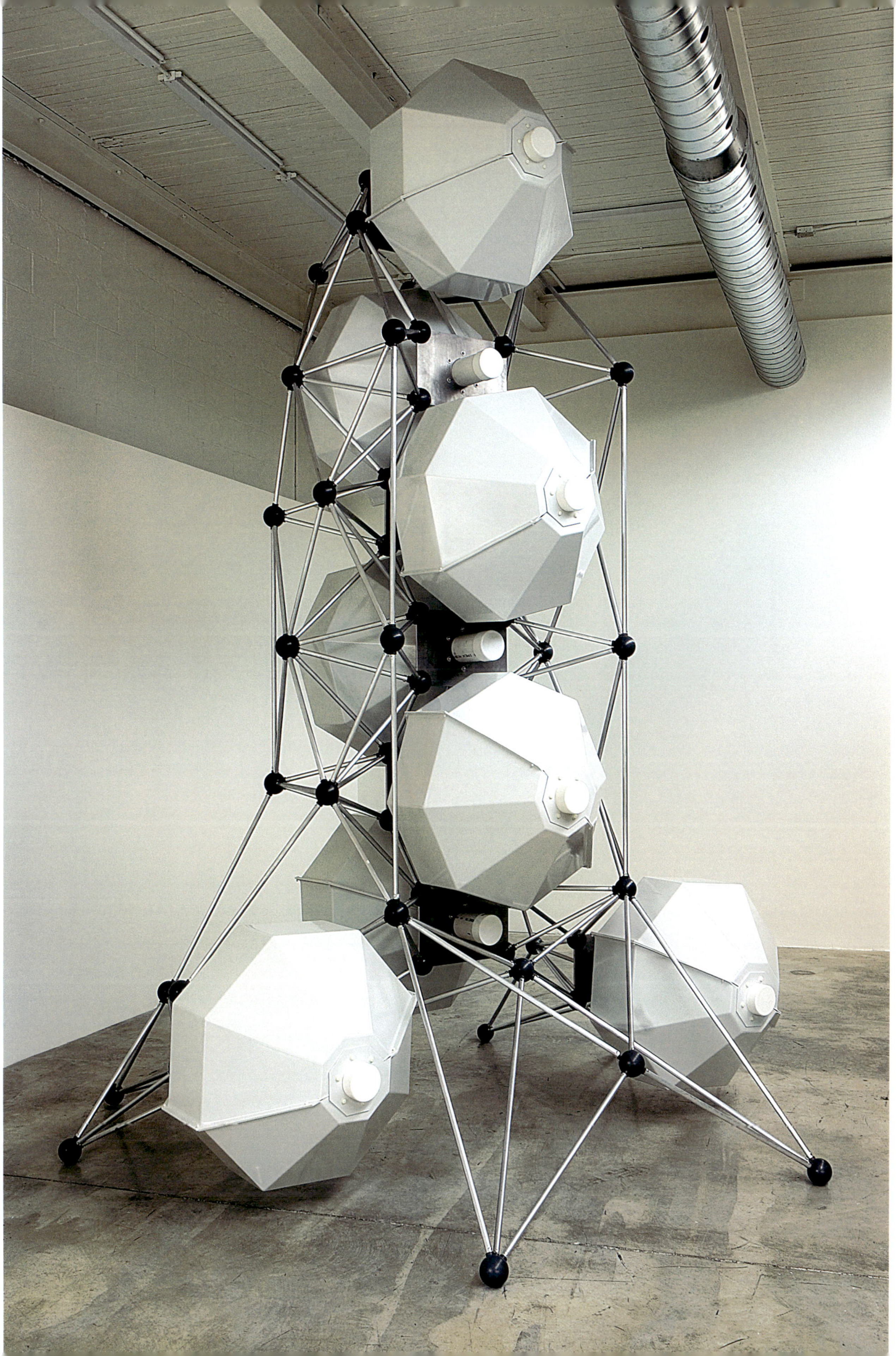

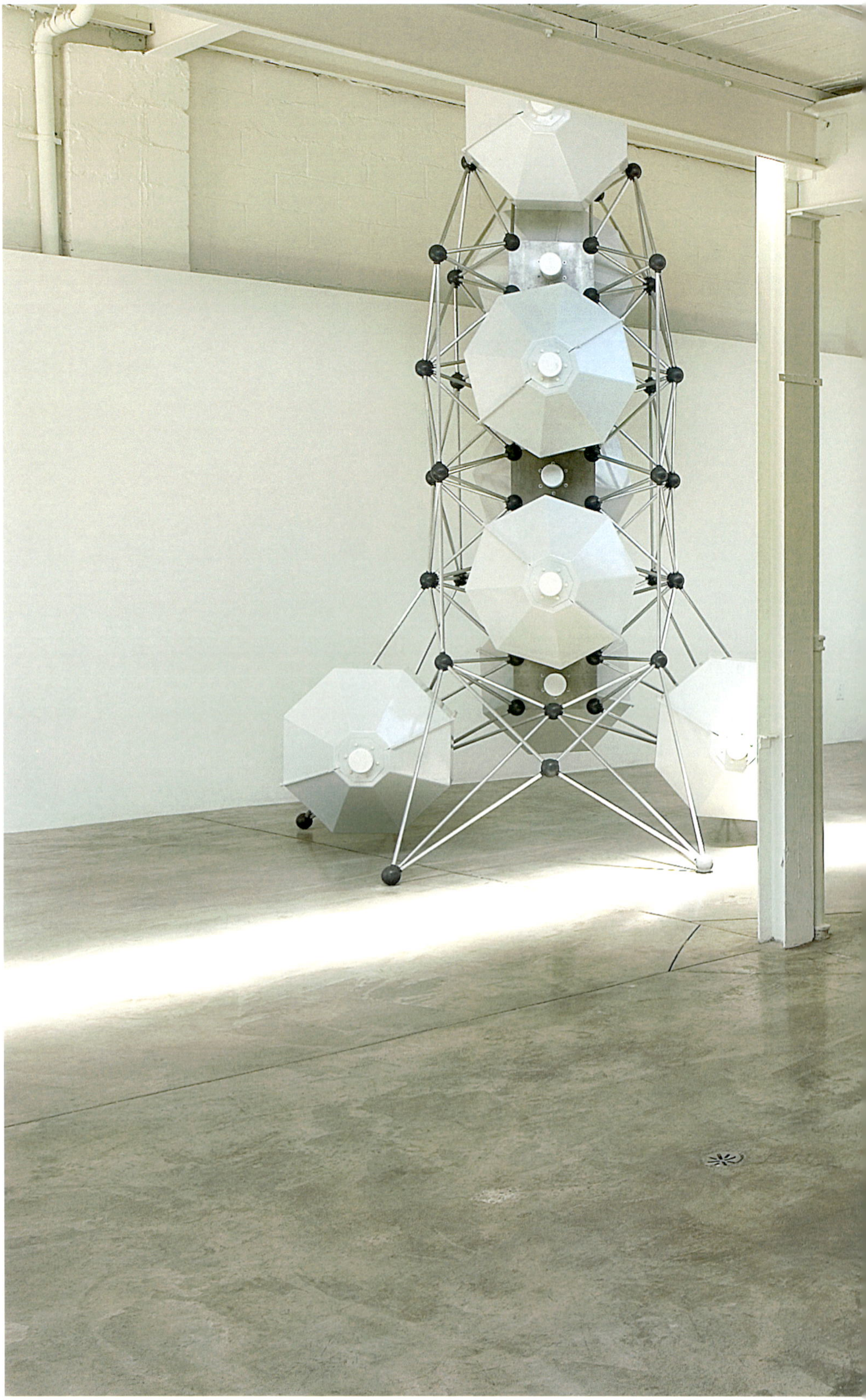

*IDCSP, Alouette and Cosmos*, 2006

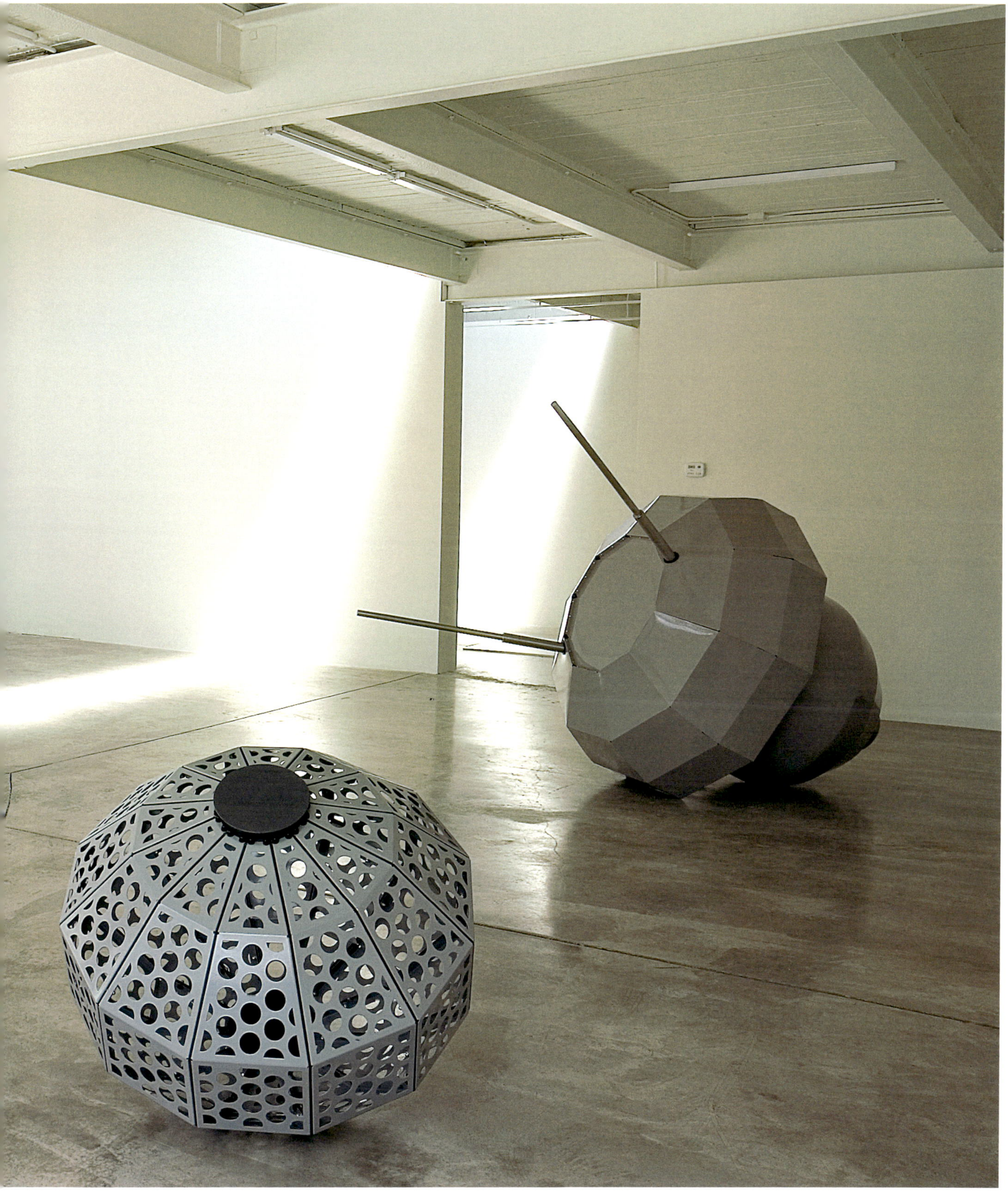

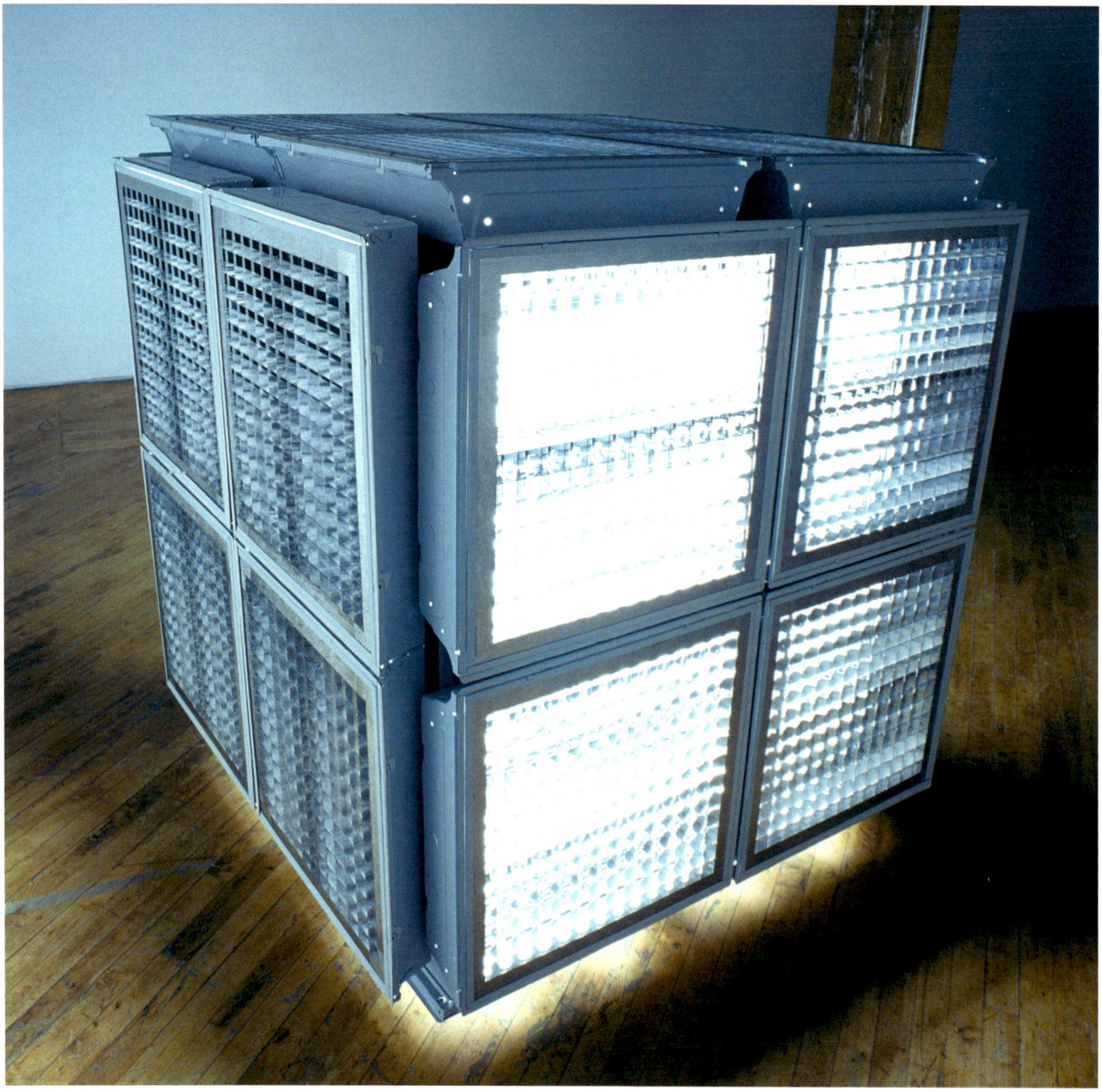

*Excel*, 2004
Fluorescent light fixtures and steel struts
122 x 122 x 132 cm

# INTRODUCTION

Daniel Young and Christian Giroux belong to a generation of contemporary artists who exist in a curious world where digital interfaces have become an inextricable part of our lives. Their adaptation of computer systems, logic, software and forms embodies a language with which they investigate our more analogue tendencies, our affection for material, form, space, and our relationship with the lingering legacy of Modernism.

Young and Giroux live in separate cities. They arrive at the final form of their sheet metal and IKEA sculptures through 3D modeling software in which they create virtual forms that are passed back and forth over email until both are satisfied. It is a "Boolean" process, of fluidly adding and subtracting elements to and from a form (IKEA furnishings in this case). These fully detailed computer drawings are then sent to an industrial fabricator, the parts assembled from sheet metal and powder coated leaving them seemingly indestructible and untouched by human hands.

As critic/historian Kenneth Hayes points out in his essay herein, sculptures such as these reference an historical moment when the machine aesthetic and Modernism take a Postmodern turn. For Young and Giroux, the aesthetic of Tony Smith, Larry Bell, and Donald Judd are conflated with Gordon Matta-Clark, Constantin Brancusi, IKEA, contemporary architecture and all the political, economic and social dimensions that permeate throughout.

Young and Giroux's adaptation of IKEA furniture and its relationship to the "infra-ordinary" is considered in a text by Jesse Huisken. He describes IKEA's cheap, mass-produced design as easily envisioned in a digital realm, "at home" and comfortable in the place it was created. Indeed, the superficial nature of the IKEA object feels all the more virtual when its flimsy innards are exposed through the cuts demanding alignment with the artists' own designs.

Mark Lanctôt further examines their practice in his essay, which positions Young and Giroux's recent sculpture *Mr. Smith* (2010) with their film, *Every Building, or Site, that a Building Permit has been Issued for a New Building in Toronto in 2006* (2008); both were featured in an exhibition at the Musée d'art contemporain de Montréal in 2011. Lanctôt reveals the artists' interest in the production of space, the built environment, and draws our attention to the overlap of Tony Smith's modular, near-architectural objects with the banal sculptural forms of contemporary urban development.

This catalogue represents the culmination of almost a decade of Young and Giroux's work in tandem with a range of thoughtful voices offering new insights, context, and a deep appreciation for an artistic practice that rigorously challenges our senses and intellect. We are very pleased to have been able to exhibit a selection of their sculpture and to have helped realize this exceptional publication.

**Ryan Doherty, Curator**
**Southern Alberta Art Gallery**

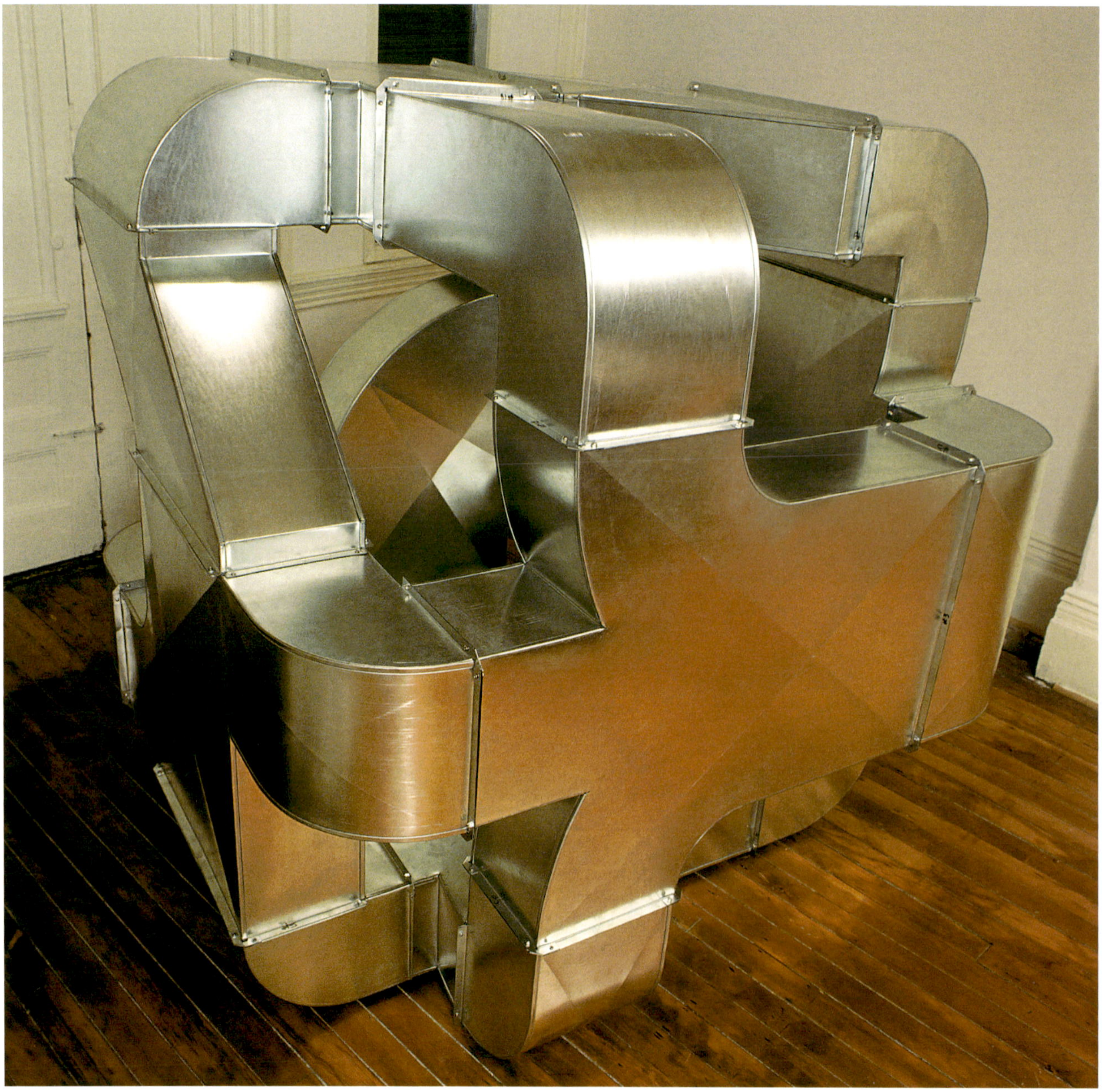

*Access*, 2004
Galvanized steel ductwork
183 x 183 x 183 cm

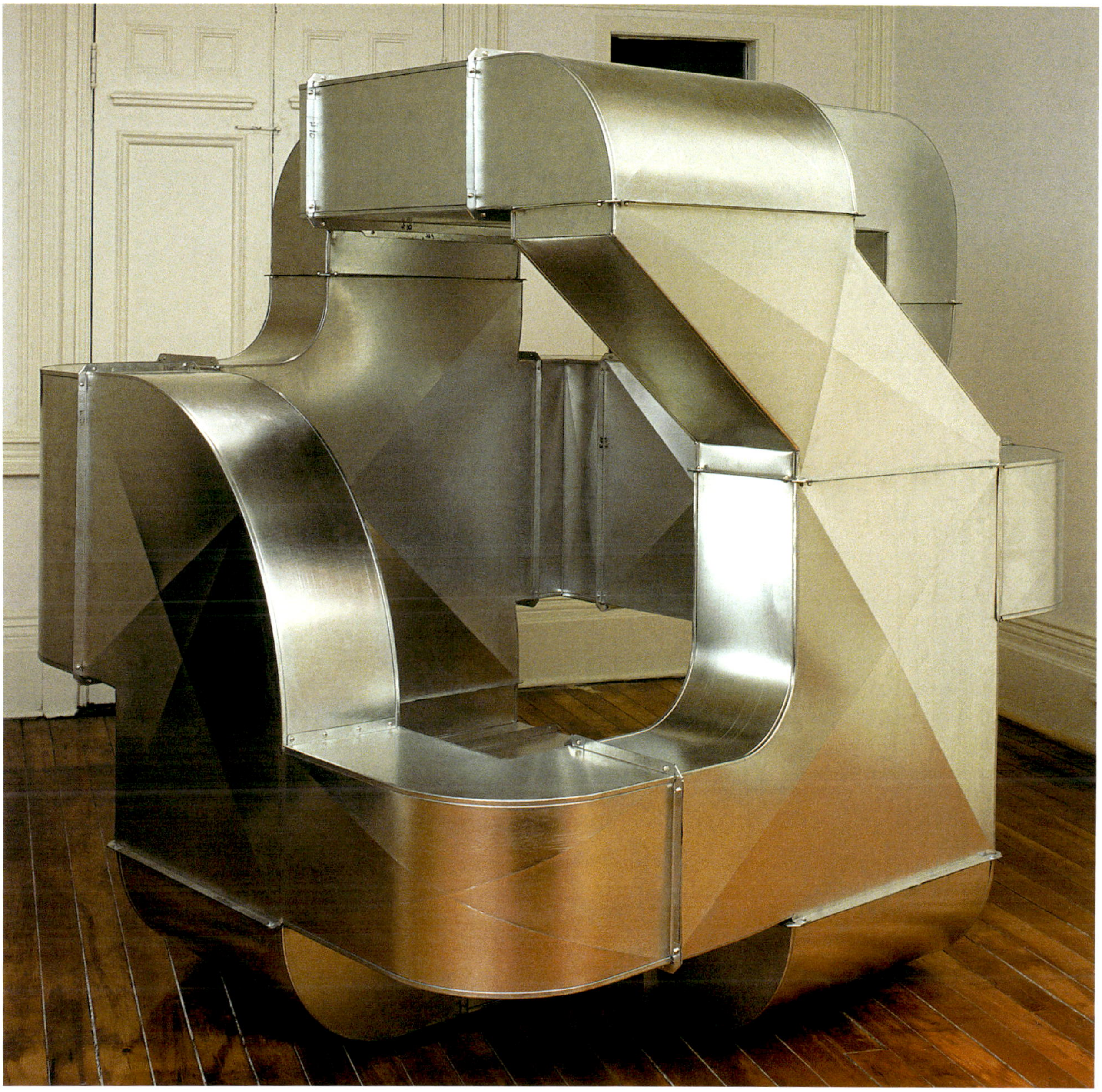

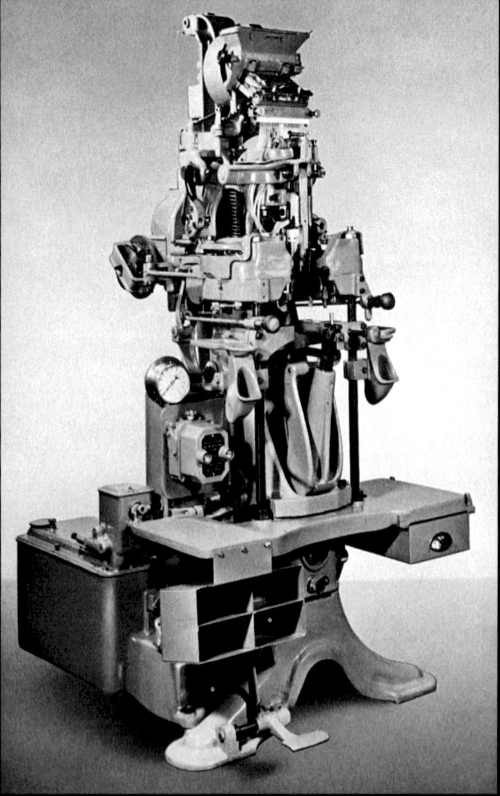

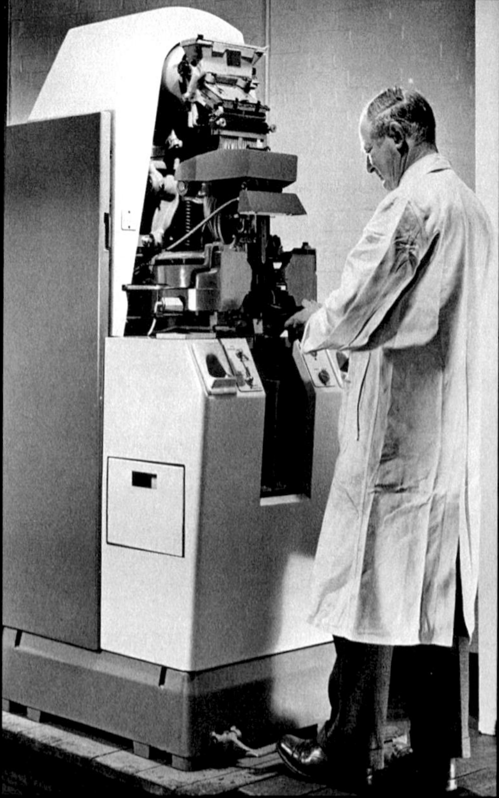

A shoemaking machine (left) – redesigned (right).

# Less is Moron

In 1968, the engineer W.H. Mayall authored an elegant little book titled *Machines and Perception in Industrial Design*, in which he identified the dangers and difficulties created for their operators by the growing complexity of modern machines. He attributed these problems, which often had disfiguring or even fatal consequences, to the multiplication of parts beyond the capacity of a worker to assimilate and respond to them appropriately. Mayall described the emergence and development of this problem in strictly historical terms, but he understood it as being fundamentally a matter of perception, or rather, of the limits to perception. He argued that simply organizing machines into coherent visual fields would aid workers in recognizing which parts could safely be handled and which could not, thus preventing accidents. In case after case, Mayall demonstrated the advantages of enclosing machines in carefully designed sheet-metal housings, showing how old machines could be refurbished to attain visual coherence and improve performance.

In the progressive spirit of Modernism, Mayall credited smartly designed machines with aiding labour's gradual advance in dignity and social status. From the present perspective, however, it appears that the enclosure of the working parts of machines had other, more profound and entirely unintended, consequences. Simple machines such as levers, screws, pulleys and gears have the virtue of being readily comprehensible, and in the modern era, the best designed and most functional machines were taken as emblems of rationality. When machines grew so complex that they had to be housed in metal cases, their operations became completely unavailable to visual analysis and understanding. Chassis, with all they connote in terms of foundation and structure, were concealed in buoyantly coloured volumes, or done away with entirely. No one can regret the reduction in the number of workers' digits lost to suddenly activated machine parts, but this improvement nevertheless cost the loss of the intellectually satisfying, axiomatic character of tools and work. The opaque housings had the unexpected effect of rendering machines not less, but rather, more mysterious. The new housings operated like a modern version of the iconostasis in the Russian Orthodox Church: a screen that, by hiding the working mechanisms, elicited wonder, projections and fantasies. In short, what machines lost in transparency they gained in the allure that emanates from all hidden and unknowable things.

These new machines certainly changed the conditions of labour, but perhaps not quite in the direction Mayall hoped. They asked of their users a fraction of the formerly requisite manual dexterity, a minimum of attention, and less alacrity. In effect, they deskilled workers, making them increasingly interchangeable and ultimately dispensable. Mayall's Pop-era workers were ideally reduced to intermittently pushing a single button on a slick, featureless box. Drudgery, alienation, and stupefying wonder merged in the enigma of the box-as-instrument, which fascinates precisely because there is nothing to see. Taken to its limit, Modernism's reductive drive results in a condition of mindless automation: Less is Moron.

By the time Mayall wrote his treatise, Modernist sculpture seemed to have definitively rejected the Brechtian edict that the work of art lay bare the means whereby the aesthetic effect is produced. Art critics and historians generally correlate this "Postmodern" turn with the abandonment of the machine as an aesthetic ideal and the repudiation of its model of transparency. The consequent displacement of (sculptural) mass by (painterly) volume in American sculpture followed a well-known course: David Smith's final *Cubi* (1961-65) series broke with orthodox, Machinic Modernism; Anne Truitt, Ronald Bladen and Tony Smith developed volume into a sculptural idiom; Donald Judd became its master and theorist; and John McCracken and Larry Bell refined the sculptural box and carried it to the shimmering heights of aesthetic perfection.

Naturally, such a dramatic change was fraught with controversy, but the notion that the path to Minimalism constituted a turning away from the machine as a model must be qualified by a recognition of the radical changes in machines that were taking place during the same time span. Late-modern artists may have become disenchanted with the rational armature and implicit movement of mechanisms as such, but they began to submit instead to the fascination exerted by their housings, which had quickly come to define the new image of the machine. Their work did not repudiate the machine; rather, it reflected a fairly sudden and drastic change that had rendered machines fabulous.

Writing his treatise at the cusp of this development, Mayall concluded the historical part of his narrative by noting that, "in many cases... electrical, hydraulic and pneumatic devices have replaced mechanical motions." He went on to ask, "How could we show in a computer's casing the function it performs?" Mayall's answer—that this could be accomplished by displaying a precision analogous to the computer's calculations—now seems trite, but no critic of design or theorist of Modernism surpassed his formulation of the historical problem. It is perhaps not surprising that many artists independently came to the same conclusion, and that an entire generation of sculptors whose work continued to engage with modern modes of production took the slickly designed, featureless box as the touchstone of their practice.

These protracted introductory remarks frame issues raised by the sculptural practice of Daniel Young and Christian Giroux. Not only have Young and Giroux developed a sculptural production based on the industrial fabrication of simple sheet-metal boxes, they also specifically locate their work in relation to the historical problems and conditions of late Modernism, in both its industrial and artistic forms. The artists declared this intention at the outset of their partnership in 2002. *Fullerene* (2003), their inaugural sculptural work, was an eight-foot-diameter sphere made of aluminum struts clad in bicycle-tire material. Modelled explicitly on Buckminster Fuller's geodesic dome (an icon of both the establishment and the counter-culture of the sixties) and named for the theoretical model of a carbon atom he predicted would be discovered, the work projected the total order of a structural system as an urban-scale toy. At once homage and a deliberate trivialization, the sphere alludes to the confounded relationship between art and function. The design sensibility heralded in *Fullerene* was explored further in the subsequent works *Access* and *Excel* (2004). Named after two of the most ubiquitous computer programs of our times, these sculptures were made of generic office space materials: HVAC ducts and fluorescent lighting fixtures. Ironically, iconically cubic, these works turned rationalism's axiomatic drive into absurd, tautological knots.

The artists' intention to make work of explicitly historical consciousness was confirmed and further elaborated in their next project, the reconstruction of a trio of satellites from the early sixties: *IDCSP*, *Cosmos*, and *Alouette* (2006). Satellites are perfect exemplars of machines that exceed our capacity to visualize their operations. In fact, their geostationary deployment does not even allow them to be observed in operation, and we tend thus to conceive of them almost as astral bodies: remote, omniscient and ethereal. Based on photographs and drawings of the

**Opposite**

*Fullerene*, 2003
Extruded aluminum, synthetic rubber tire, aluminum plate and fasteners
244 cm in diameter

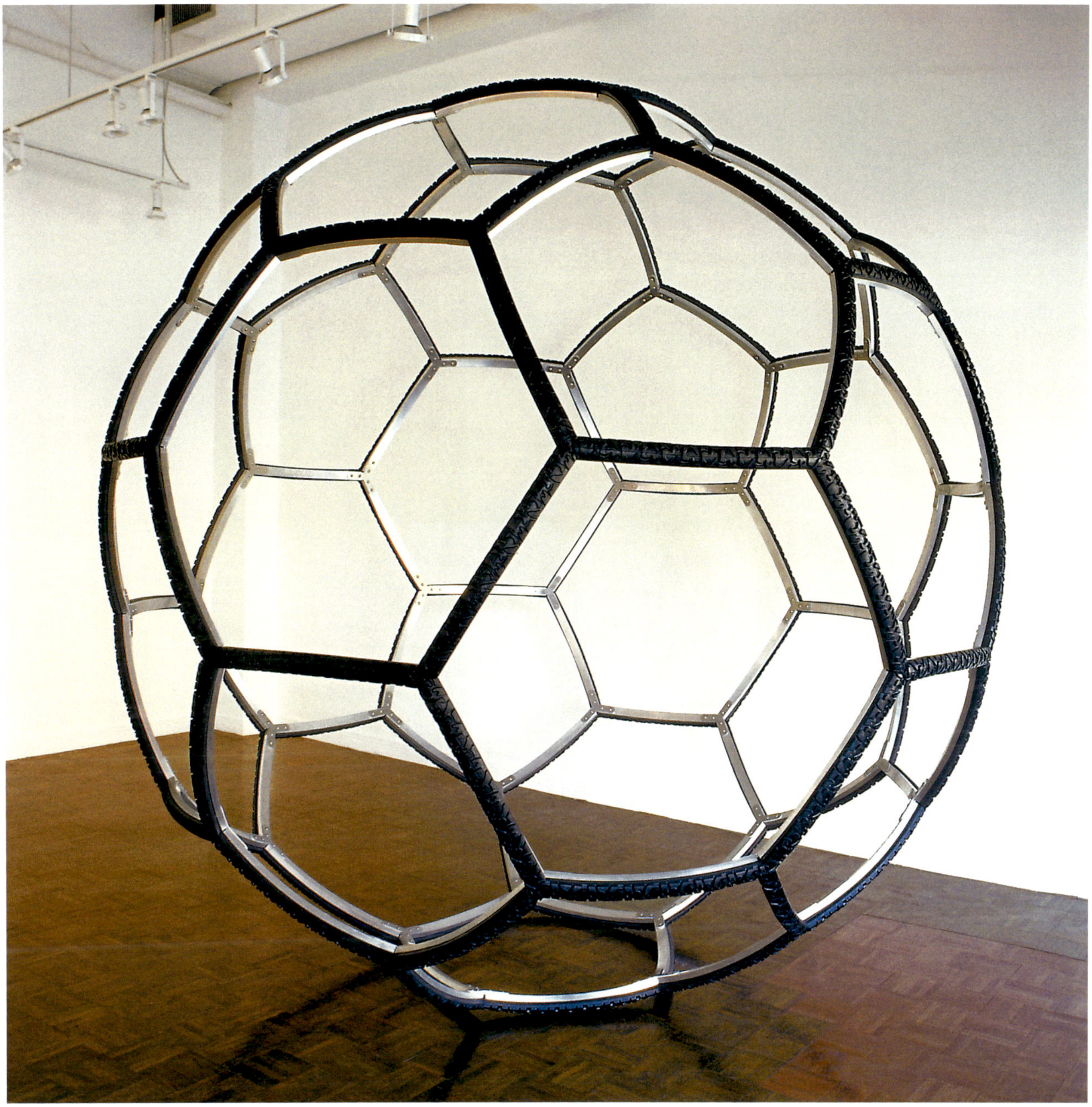

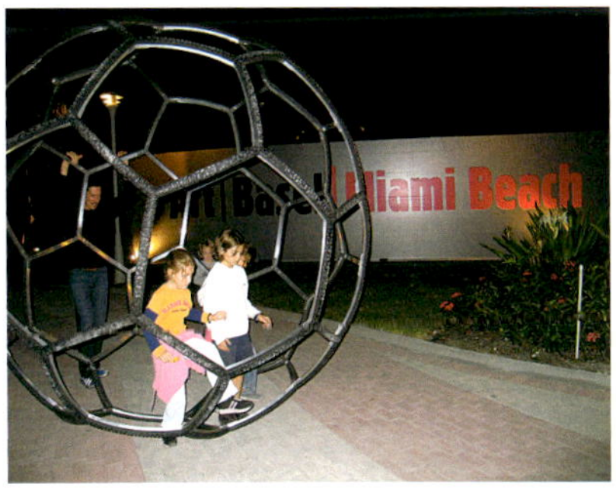

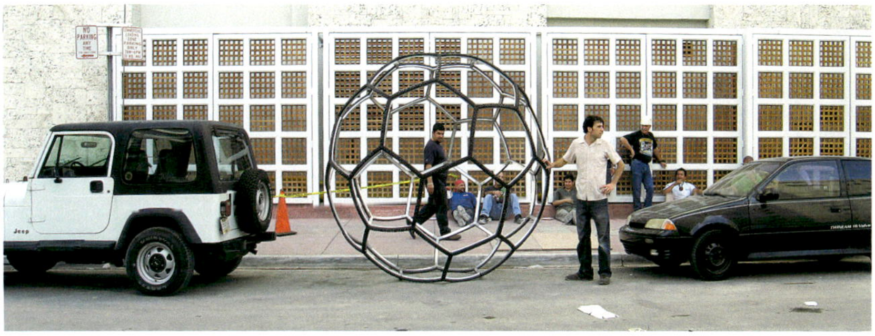

satellites, the three sculptures produced by Young and Giroux are hollow replicas of the originals. Although accepting the impossibility of a functional reconstruction, the artists nevertheless remained faithful to the originals in scale and spirit. As shells without viscera, the sculptures immediately declare the artists' abiding interests to be volume, surface and modularity—precisely those features and qualities of form that had commanded the interest of the avant-garde in the 1960s.

In addition to establishing a carefully calculated parallel with Minimalist sculpture, the portentous choice to present American, Soviet and Canadian satellites identifies the work as a reflection on the politics of the Cold-War era. This suite of satellites resonates particularly strongly with John McCracken's sculptures of the sixties—his resolutely mute, colourful and impeccably finished fiberglass planks and boxes—which, as he later revealed, he had conceived as "alien beacons" designed to attract and communicate with extraterrestrial life. For Young and Giroux, the satellites are also locational devices, designed to position both themselves and the spectator as fellow travellers in the superpower drama. The satellite works, like *Fullerene*, provide the epic framework in which the artists conceive their practice.

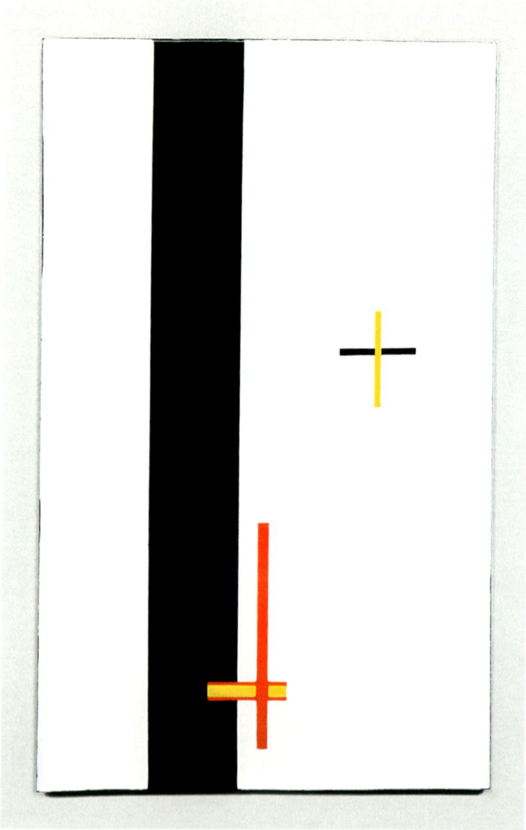

László Moholy-Nagy
*Construction in Enamel 2*, 1923
*Gift of Philip Johnson in memory of Sibyl Moholy-Nagy. The Museum of Modern Art, New York*
*© ARS, NY*

In making the satellites, Young and Giroux employed numerous industrial techniques—sheet metal fabrication, vacuum forming, CNC milling, etc. The works were designed with computer models that were sent to industrial facilities as digital files. This method allowed the artists to interact with industrial fabrication on its own terms. For their part, the fabricators did not need to regard this work as unusual or especially precious, as it was neither more nor less difficult than their routine tasks. This mode of production recalls Moholy-Nagy's provocative 1921 suite of telephone paintings, which were designed on graph paper and communicated by telephone to sign makers who then executed the works in fired enamel on metal panels. All of Young and Giroux's sculpture reveals barely a trace of handwork and the final results often look uncannily like the original computer renderings. In fact, the sculptures are never fully assembled until they arrive at the exhibition space. The artists thus effectively transform the industrial shop into a studio, and their exhibitions tend to transform the look and feel of the gallery into that of the warehouse.

Young and Giroux retained this cool, remote working method for subsequent sculptural productions. The satellites required a survey of available productive means, which the artists focused and refined in a deeper engagement with sheet-metal fabrication in an ongoing series of works that incorporate furniture made for and sold by IKEA. In place of their earlier, overtly historicizing practice of reconstruction, the artists now took up actual commodities produced and consumed in contemporary society. By so doing, their sculptures began to manifest an unavoidable affinity with the Surrealist notion of the condensation of two heterogeneous realities. The realities that collide in these new works, however, are not particularly heterogeneous; there is, for example, none of the animistic ambition of Victor Brauner, whose *Wolf Table* (1939-47) imbued a simple piece of furniture with atavistic resemblances (except,

**Opposite**

Victor Brauner
*Loup-table (Wolf Table)*, 1939-47
*Musée National d'Art Moderne, Centre Georges Pompidou, Paris, France*
*© ARS, NY*

Christopher Williams
*Cutaway model Switar 25 mm f1.4. AR. Glass, wood and brass. Photography by the Douglas M. Parker Studio, Glendale, California, November 17, 2007 - November 30, 2007*, 2008
*Courtesy of David Zwirner, New York*

perhaps, in the green sculpture titled *Kermit* [2006]). The IKEA furniture is sufficiently familiar and banal to stand for things in general, although the specific pieces sometimes evoke stage flats, podia or vitrines, i.e., the furniture of institutional rather than domestic spaces. Standing in place of the armature in classical sculpture or the chassis of traditional machines, the furniture renders the artists' lacerations, alterations, additions and incorporations highly legible. It is not easily decided whether the artists' intention in working with consumer items is to infiltrate the productive system or to adulterate its products. There is, however, a certain cunning audacity in confronting furniture—one of sculpture's *bêtes noires*—so directly, and Young and Giroux have done so in a way that avoids the cloying effects sometimes evident in the work of Ian Carr-Harris, Rachel Whiteread, Doris Salcedo and Ai Wei Wei, among others.

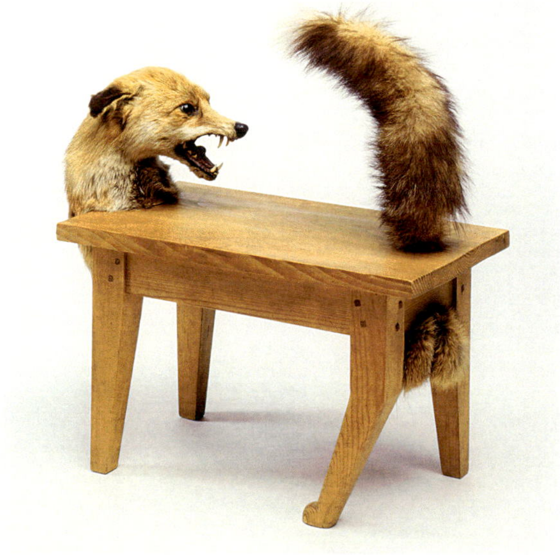

The cut or slash is one of the strongest features in the IKEA works. Some critics have likened this gesture to the cuts in buildings made by Gordon Matta-Clark, but the notion of disrupting the oppressively seamless fabric of reality was ubiquitous in the art of the Conceptual era, where the cut served as a sign of resistance to the totality of "the system." Some prominent examples of this are Lawrence Weiner's self-explanatory *A Square Removal from a Rug in Use* (1969) and Richard Serra's *Cutting Device: Base Plate Measure* (1969), in which, enacting the anecdote of the Procrustean bed, Serra reduced heterogeneous materials to the length of an underlying steel plate.

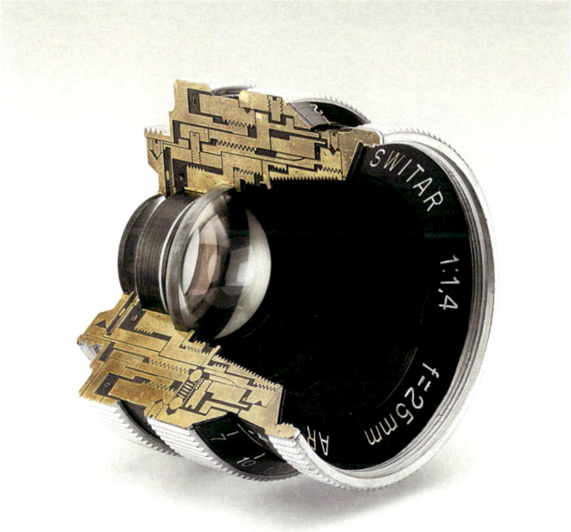


Young and Giroux use the cut in a distinctly different way, one that indicates the dissimilarities between then and now. The ordinary function of a cut in the fabric of an object is to provide a rational perspective that reveals the order hidden within—like a plan or section. Section lines usually follow an object's ordinates precisely in order to reveal as much as possible of the object's constitution. This is how, for example, the sectional cut functions in a series of photographs by Christopher Williams. In *Cutaway model Switar 25mm f1.4 AR...* (2008), Williams photographed a camera lens to show its surprisingly complex internal workings. For all its simplicity—it would not be out of place in a technical manual—this seemingly objective picture tends to mythologize the camera, almost attributing to it an inner life. Its optical self-referentiality is rather like that of the famous photograph by Paul Strand of a New York City beggar wearing a sign declaring her *BLIND* (1916), or of the infamous slashed eyeball in Luis Buñuel's *Un Chien Andalou* (1928). Young and Giroux's cuts make no claim to reveal the essence of the appropriated objects. They do expose the invariably flimsy construction and material impoverishment of IKEA furniture, but this is hardly news. The cuts exhibit no particularly analytical character, and no obvious principle of organization or distribution; they perform no major dissections, and hardly seem adequate as an exposé. Odd to say, the cuts do not even seem invasive. Their character is emblematic, and they seem to relate to the idiom of folding and incising that pervades contemporary art and design. The sculptors' use of the term "Boolean" to reference this entire body of work supports this reading. Indeed, the procedure of excising and adding volumes expresses a restless, experimental mapping or some sort of informational probing rather than a philosophical drive to penetrate to the heart of the matter.

The identical elements in many of the sculptures are frequently differentiated by colour, in much the same way that mass-produced consumer goods are customized to provide the appearance of choice. Like the excisions themselves, the powder coating betrays not the slightest sign of labour and, needless to say, colour is never mixed. Each component in a work always maintains its individual, minimally customized identity. This feature of the work might be a legacy of Giroux's former painting practice, but it also responds simply and effectively to the need to finish sheet metal in some way. Regardless of its origins, the application of paint pointedly disclaims any notion of material expression. The ethos is Suprematist or Neo-plastic rather than Constructivist. Indeed, it is not inconceivable that the same forms could have been made in plastic and integrally coloured.

In a number of the gridded works, the applied colour functions almost like pixels, suggesting a highly magnified view of a rasterized image. The apparently random distribution of colour often dazzles the eye; like Mayall's distracted worker, one does not know where to look. This is especially the case with the series of sculptures titled *Andersson* (2010), where the applied colour makes it difficult to determine precisely how many different components have been added to each of the IKEA stepstools in the cluster, or, for that matter, whether each component is unique. The total effect is akin to witnessing one of those colour-coded models of DNA, broken into short, free-floating bits. The work reads like a sign of an intellect at work, straining to comprehend a structure just beyond its capacity. There is also something genomic about the grid of metal boxes on top of and beneath an L-shaped desk in the enigmatically titled *Jjimjilbang* (2010). The boxes seem to multiply like a colour-coded desk organizer that has metastasized to engulf the whole.

Salient among the current work is *Brave New Waves* (2010), which appears as something of a return to earlier themes. A large, black, IKEA bookshelf/room divider filled with metal boxes that make the whole virtually solid, the sculpture is rendered in four shades of grey from near-white to near-black; it is also square and gridded, as were *Excel* and *Access*. The apparently arbitrary disposition of the tones invites one to mentally shuffle them into grey-scale order. The artists' characteristic excisions are restricted to one face, which the viewer is phenomenologically inclined to identify as the back. Here the sculptors come close to mimicking the unmistakable scale and dramatic spatial disposition of classic Minimalist sculpture. In doing so, they have declared their affinity for a subject-object form of relational dynamics antecedent to the interpersonal ones currently *en vogue*.

From an early point in their collaboration, the artists have presented their ideas for larger sculptural works and outdoor installations in the form of computer-generated images and finely crafted maquettes. *Reticulated Gambol* (2007-08), a sculpture located in Lee Centre Park in suburban Toronto, is the artists' first realized public commission. Bearing all the hallmarks of the artists' method (i.e., industrial fabrication, a code-like structure and brilliant monochrome colour), the work consists of a matrix of standard CSA-certified playground equipment—curved ladders, tubes, shallow bridges, tall arches and helical poles —fixed in a bed of sand. The entire structure is painted bright blue. Although the "gambol" of the title refers to frolicking, it is also a homonym for "gamble," and cryptically alludes to the taking of risks. The sculpture was designed in accordance with the very stringent safety parameters that apply to playground structures. Essentially a labyrinth (the game of snakes and ladders is the closest analogue to its precise balance of grid and curves), the structure is both liberating and harrowing—it offers a safe place to play with experiences of confinement and deterrence. The work performs a *reductio ad absurdum* of the public safety paradigm, resulting in something that feels subversive and even a bit dangerous. Following the letter of the law but not its spirit, *Reticulated Gambol* offers a glimpse of the strange, radical possibilities of unfreedom. Young and Giroux proudly note that it is the only public artwork in Toronto that is also recognized and used as an official play structure.

**Opposite**

*Reticulated Gambol*, 2007-08
Powder coated steel
1219 x 1280 x 457 cm

TORONTO

*Commissioned by the City of Toronto under the Art and Landscape collaboration program*

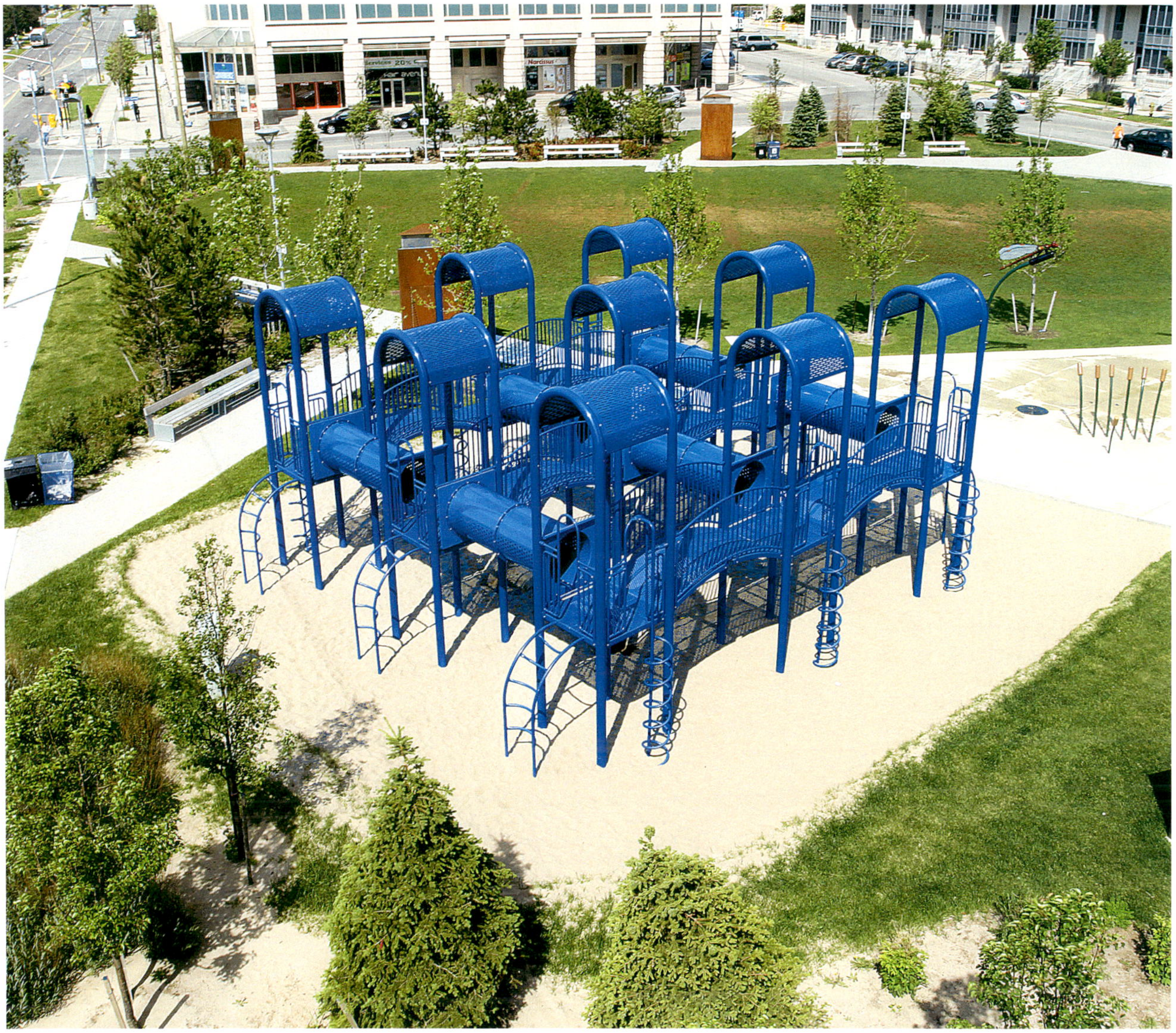

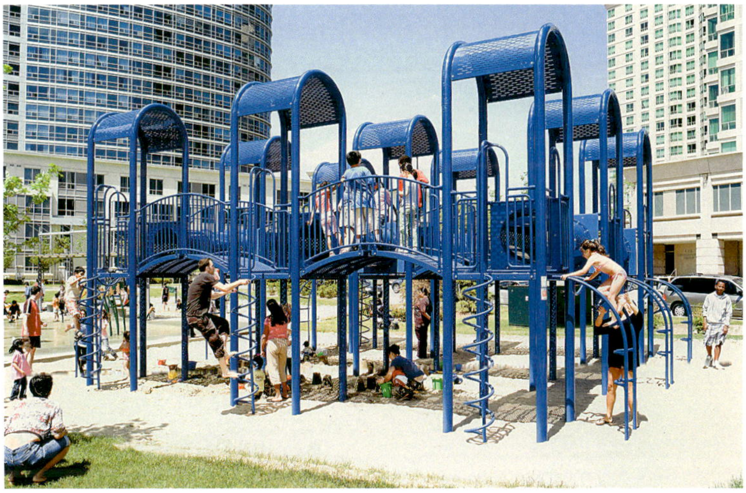

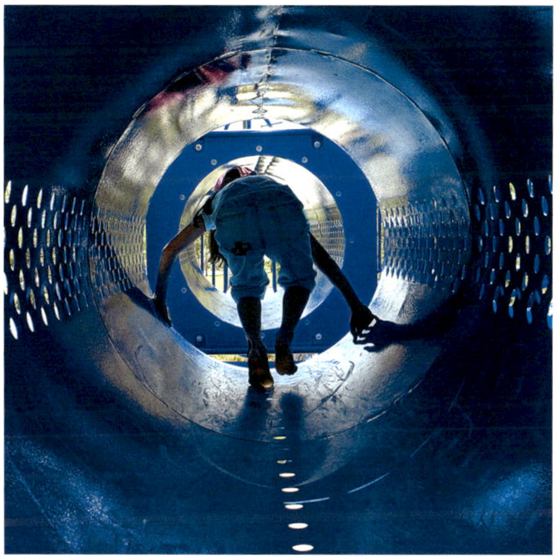

The artists' engagement with suburban space in their first public sculpture was not incidental; at the same time that they were realizing *Reticulated Gambol*, Young and Giroux also made their first 35mm motion-picture film, which surveys predominantly suburban development. Not surprisingly, their films are as rigorously preconceived and as dispassionately executed as their sculptures. The camera remains perfectly still, expunging any trace of facture or opportunity for subjective identification. In their films as much as their sculptures, it is the idea that makes the work.

Silent, thirteen minutes long and shot in colour, *Every Building, or Site, that a Building Permit was Issued for a New Building in Toronto in 2006* (2008) has been presented both in theatrical venues and as a loop on a vintage projector in galleries. The film's obvious referent is Ed Ruscha's photographic survey *Every Building on the Sunset Strip* (1966, ongoing), but the artists also see the work in relation to N.E. Thing Co.'s *Portfolio of Piles* (1969); significantly, the common denominator of these works is the interest in depicting the totality of a spatial and material system.

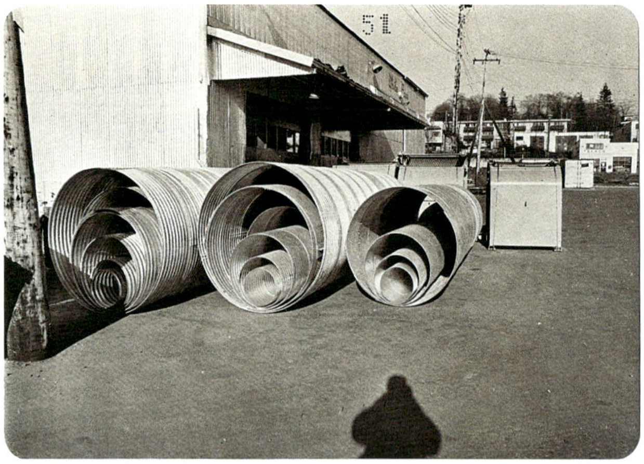


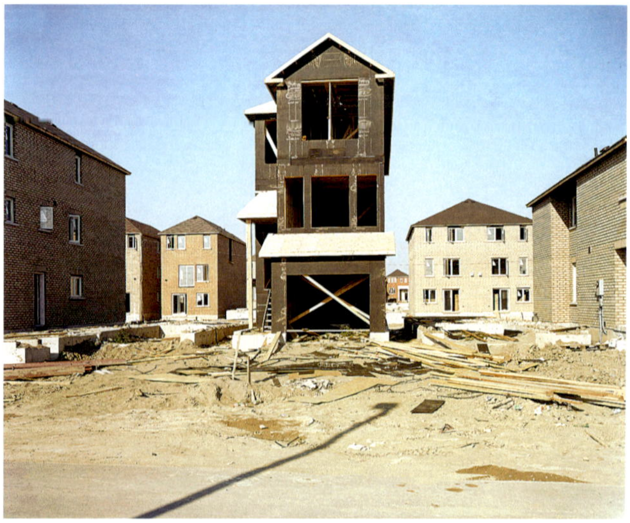

The parameters "Building permit / Toronto / 2006" produced 115 sites, each of which was filmed for eight seconds with the camera positioned to provide an oblique view of the completed building where it was possible, or a frontal view where it was not. The results are presented without titles or explanatory material. Although narrowly a documentary, the film eschews the conventional narrative or acculturating tendencies of documentaries. Whereas Geoffrey James's photographs of Toronto's suburbs, for example, present rampant development as a portent of ruination, Young and Giroux's work betrays neither satisfaction nor dismay. Indeed, the parade of images—one beige box after another, ad infinitum—induces something closer to ennui than, for example, the spatially "trippy" effects of Google Earth's street view. The clinical gaze of *Every Building...* is truly radical in its silence about the production and consumption of space. Was the work conceived as an objective indictment of modern technology's proclivity to treat nature as a standing reserve? Possibly. But if the film is a protest, its silence seems somehow self-incriminating.

This impassive investigation of the spatial production system is interiorized in the artists' film, *50 Light Fixtures from Home Depot* (2010). Identical in all major technical aspects to the earlier film, this work focuses on a small studio-built room, into which the fifty light fixtures are inserted one by one and filmed for ten seconds apiece. The room matches the film frame's aspect ratio and, although nothing is moving here, the flash of each new lamp and its sudden disapperance highlights the persistence of vision that underlies the cinematic illusion of movement. The film can be understood as an inversion of Sol Lewitt's masterful photographic work, *A Cube photographed by Carol Huebner using nine light sources and all their combinations* (1990). In Young and Giroux's film, it is the commodity—the light source itself—rather than the subjective positions that changes. Another apposite comparison can be made with Michael Vahrenwald's photographic series *Winter Landscapes* (2006), which presents doctor-prescribed depression therapy lights against a neutral grey studio backdrop. Of course, Young

N.E. Thing Co.
*Portfolio of Piles*, 1969
*Collection of the Morris and Helen Belkin Art Gallery, The University of British Columbia*

Geoffrey James
*Langstaff Road and Dufferin Street, Vaughan*, 1999
*Courtesy of the artist*

**Opposite**

*Every Building, or Site, that a BuildingPermit was Issued for a New Building in Toronto in 2006*, 2008 (frame scans)
35mm colour motion picture film (1:1.85), no sound, 13 min looping film installation

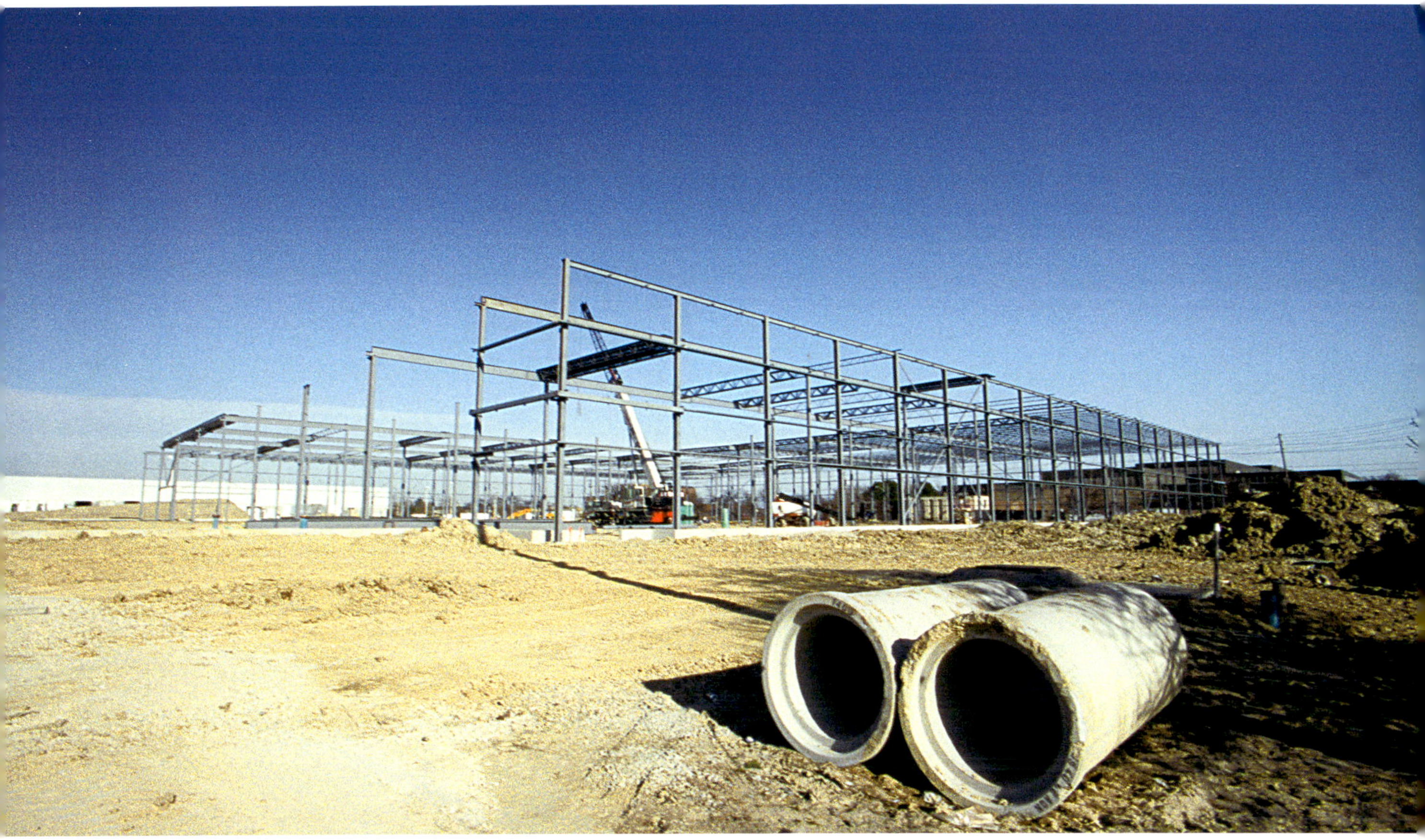

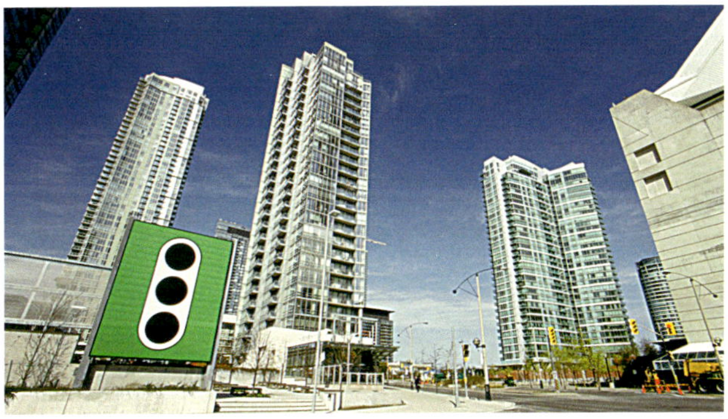

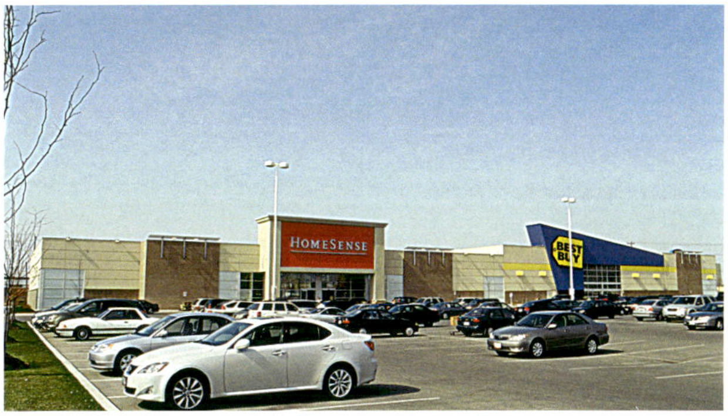
HOMESENSE
BEST BUY

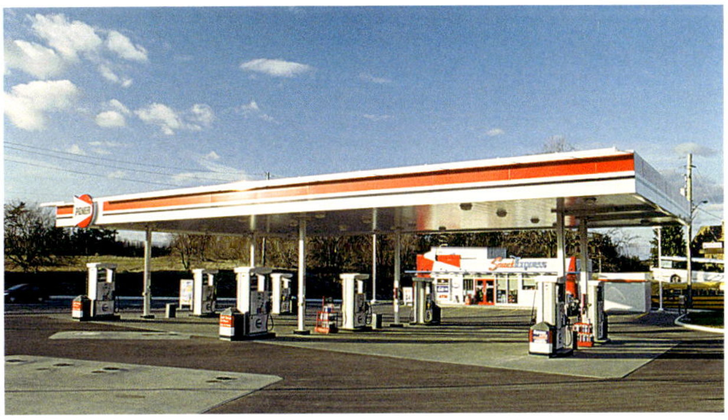

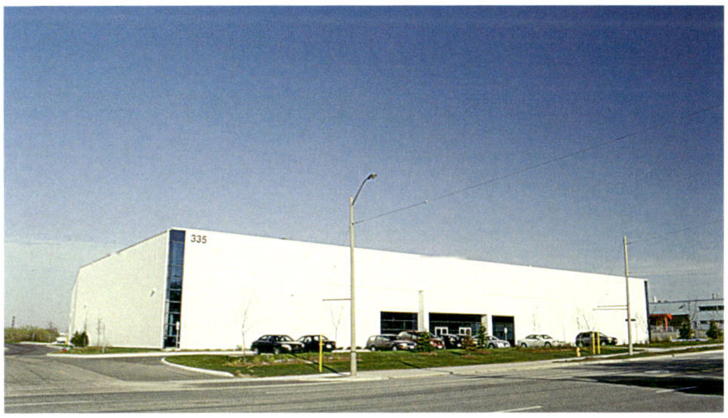
335

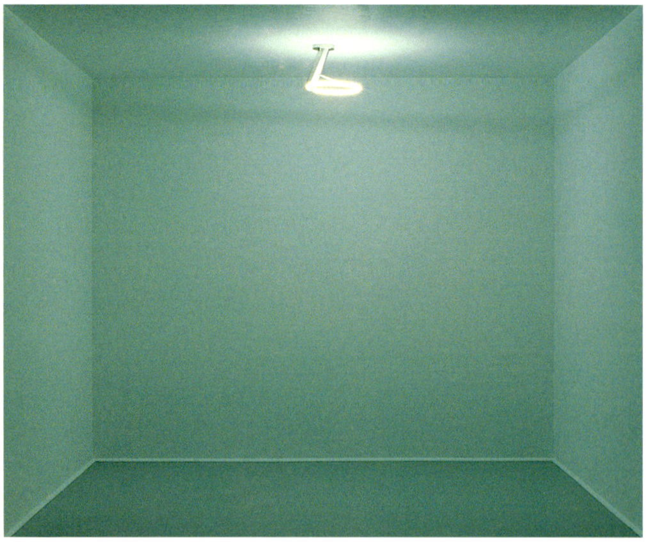
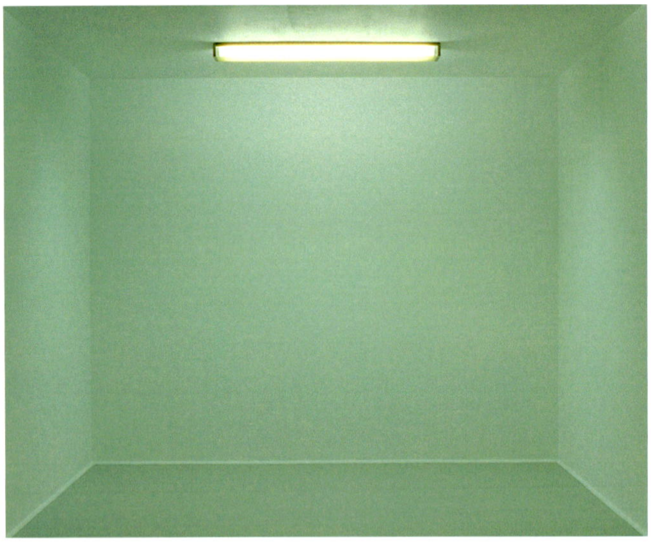
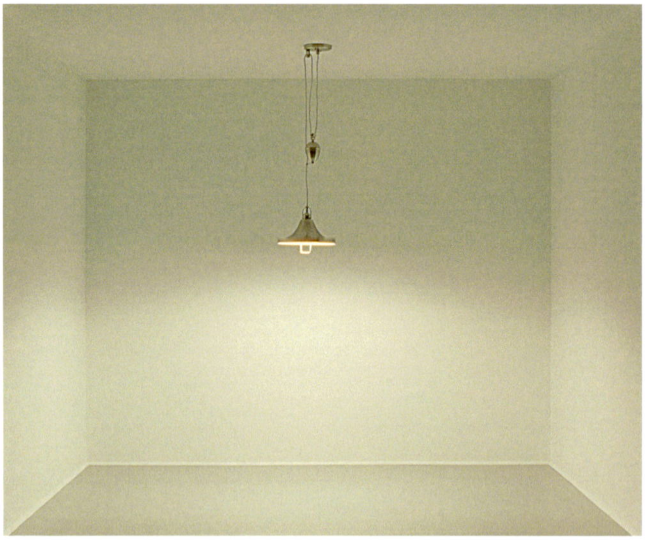

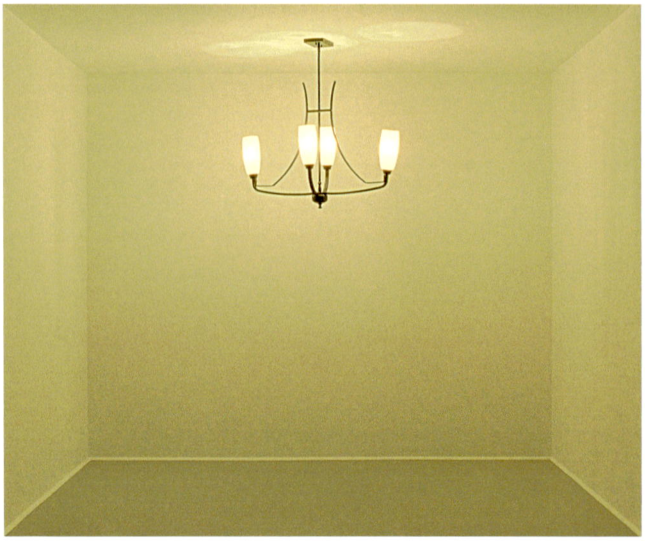

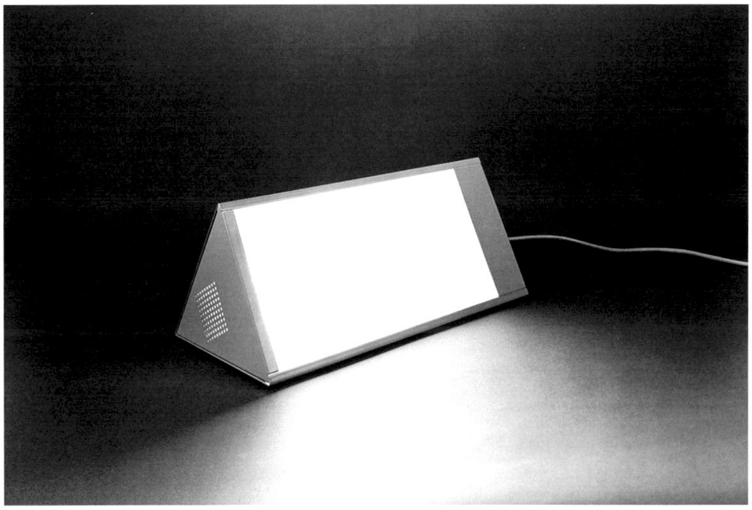

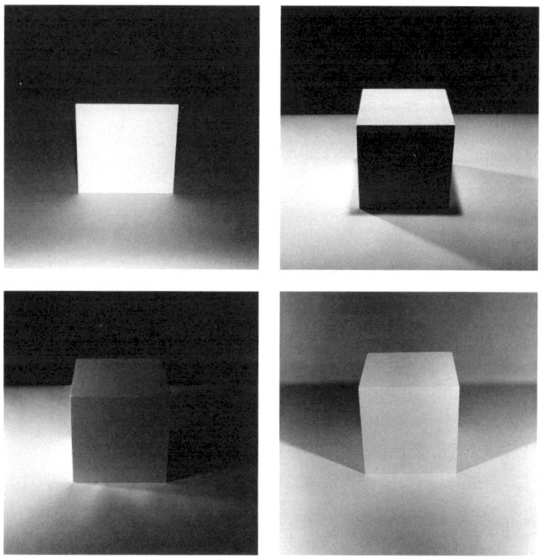

Michael Vahrenwald
*Sunlight Jr.*, 2006
*Courtesy of the artist*

Sol LeWitt
*A Cube photographed by Carol Huebner using nine light sources and all their combinations*, 1990 (four stills)
*Courtesy of Paula Cooper Gallery, New York*

**Opposite**

*50 Light Fixtures from Home Depot*, 2009 (frame scans)
35mm colour motion picture film (1:1.33), no sound, 9 min looping film installation
304 x 243 cm fixed projection size

and Giroux's work is not as openly allegorical as Vahrenwald's, but it is tempting to conclude that their restless productive procedure was employed to stave off depression. So complete is *50 Light Fixture*'s air of objectivity that it is easy to imagine finding its exact semblance on an interior-design website of the type that allows viewers to insert different options into a standard image of an interior. The film seems to enact the nesting impulse of an automaton, but in the end it neither supports the consumerist fantasy of an infinite plasticity and surplus of choice, nor does it reduce all choice to cynical indifference. It simply says that what you see is what you see.

Young and Giroux's achievement to date is the apparently contradictory one of having consistently eschewed judgement—both aesthetic and moral—in their work while retaining a sense of probity. Although they often employ strategies of radical reduction familiar from the legacies of Minimalism in sculpture and Structuralism in film, Young and Giroux are not interested in phenomenological presence, artistic purity or essences of any sort. Historical consciousness, not timeless beauty, is their goal, and they seek it by reflecting Modernism's relentless productive drive back upon itself.

KENNETH HAYES

*Kenneth Hayes is an architectural historian and a curator and critic of contemporary art. His first book of art criticism, titled* Milk and Melancholy, *was published by Prefix ICA and MIT Press in 2009.*

### Work Cited

Mayall, W.H. *Machines and Perception in Industrial Design*. London: Studio Vista Ltd; New York: Reinhold Book Corporation, a subsidiary of Chapman-Reinhold, Inc (1968).

*Hayes House* is a model for a permanent public sculpture. Situated near the crest of a hill, the piece is a steel tube outline of a geometric, modernist house. It sits directly on a walking trail so that hikers physically pass through the work as they ascend the hill. This project merges two divergent landscape practices—the private modernist villa and the public park.

**Opposite**

*Hayes House (Landscape Proposal for a Public Park)*, 2005 (detail)
Maquette
50 x 76 x 45 cm

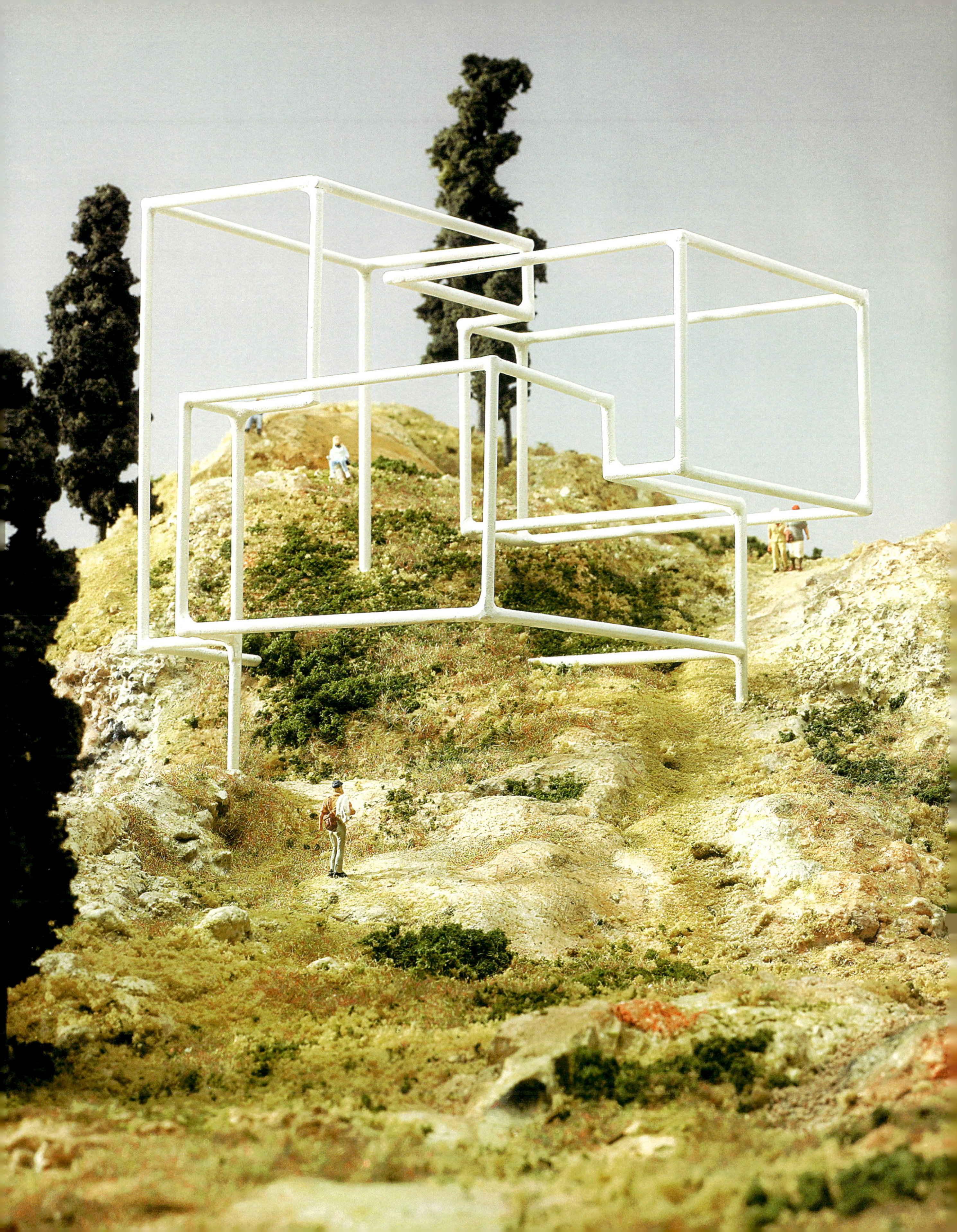

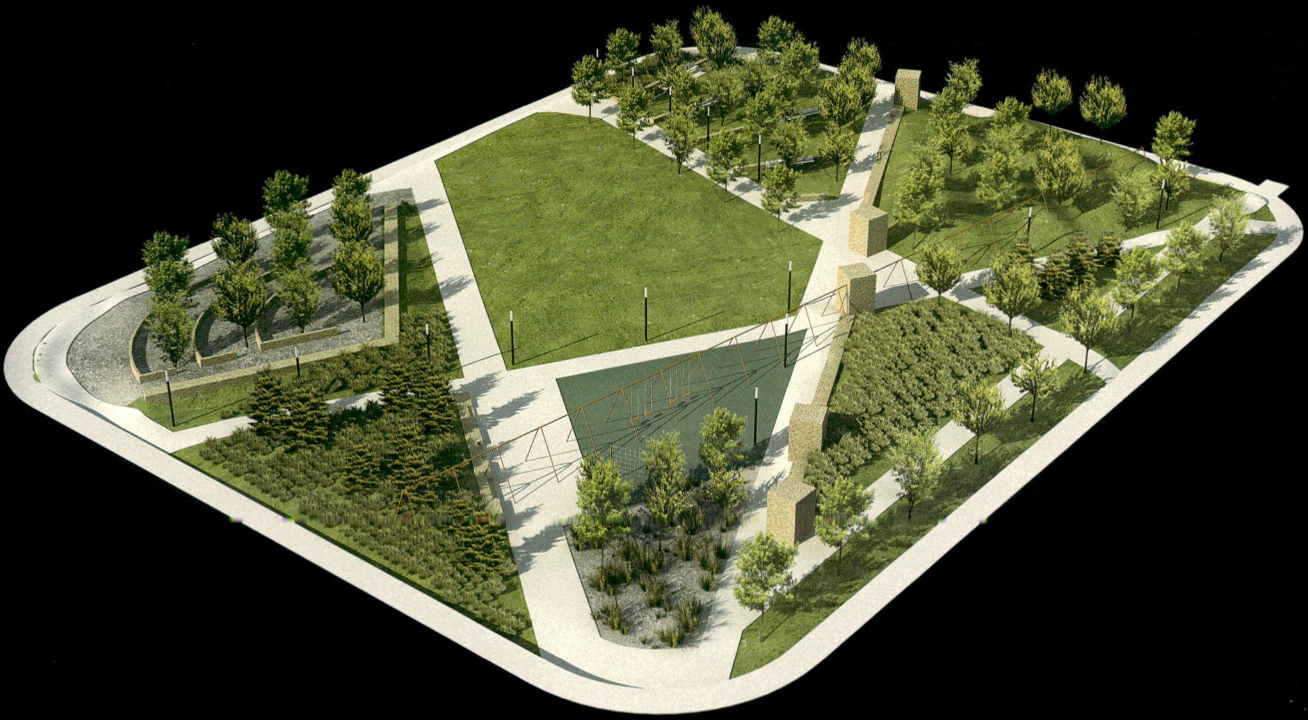

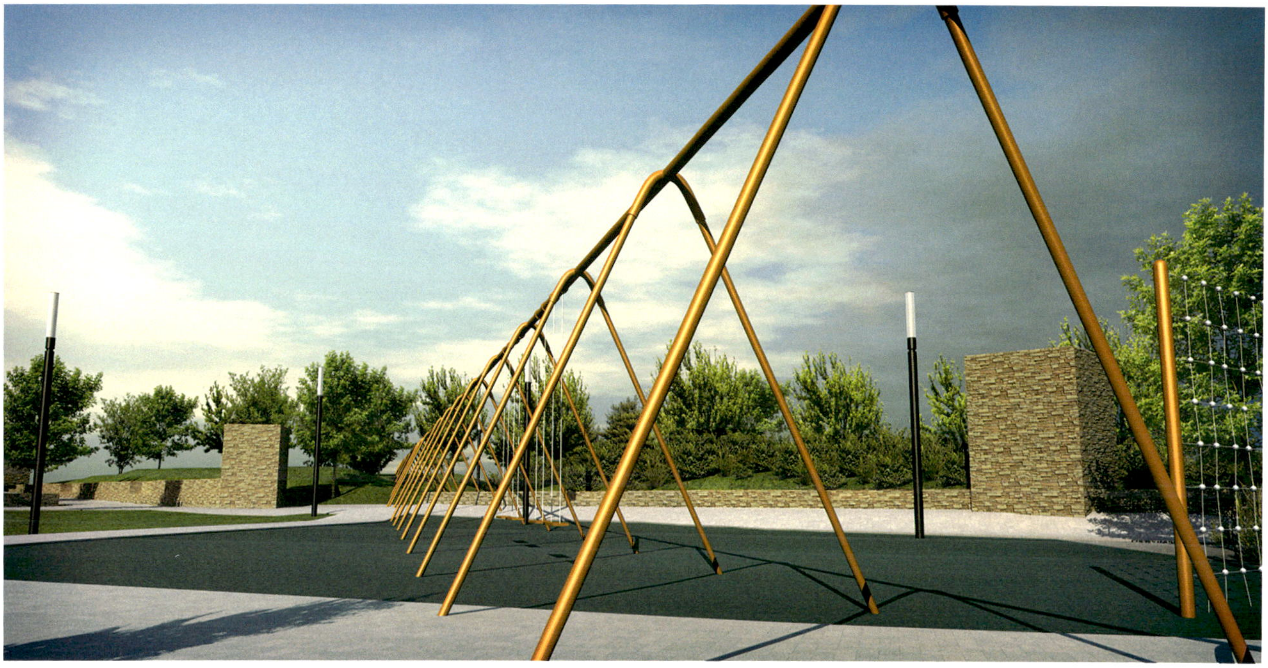

*Proposal A*, is a standard A-frame swing set extended as an archway that cuts across the length of the park along a diagonal trajectory. The top tube remains level as the grade of the park crests and slopes. In the centre of the park, where it crosses the children's play area, it becomes a functional swing. Originally intended for Lee Center Park, Toronto, *Proposal A* later developed into *Reticulated Gambol* (p 23).

*Proposal A*, 2007 (detail)
Powder coated steel
Digital rendering

**Opposite**

*Proposal A*, 2007
*Park design concept by PMA Landscape Architecture*

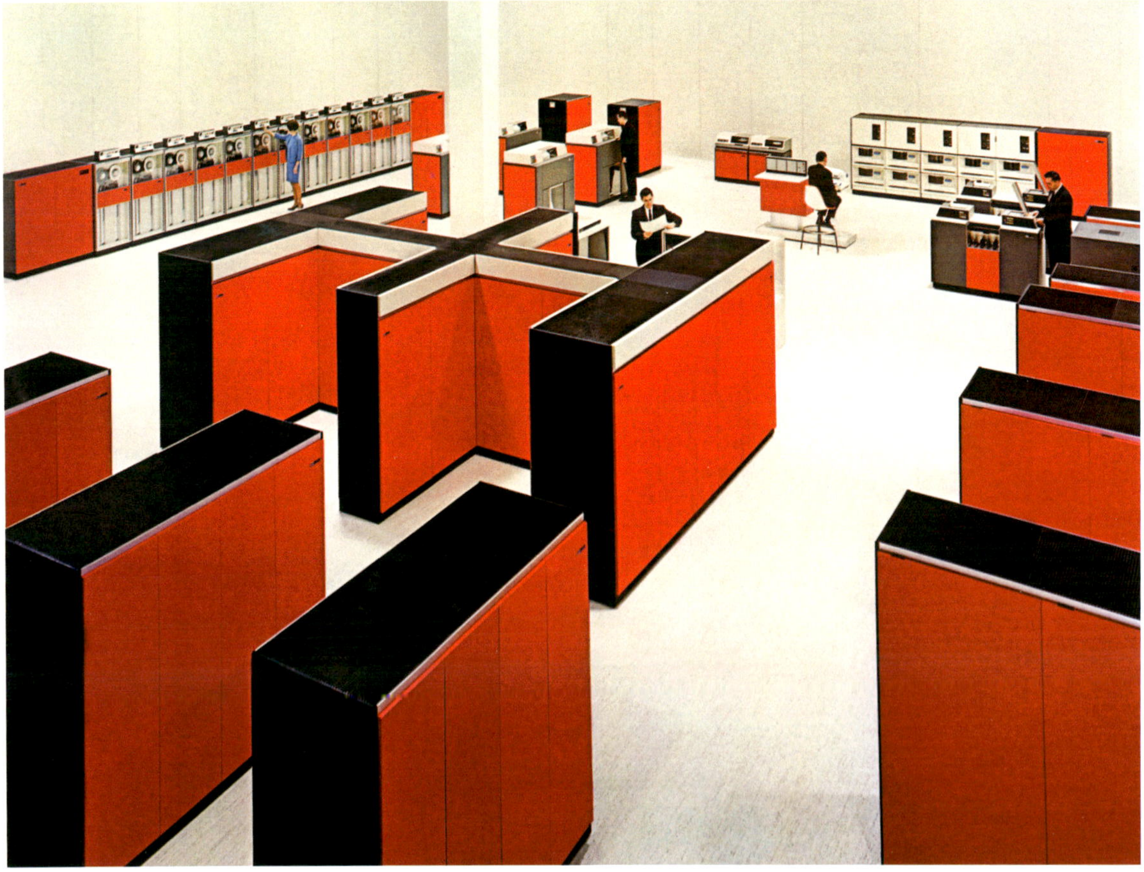

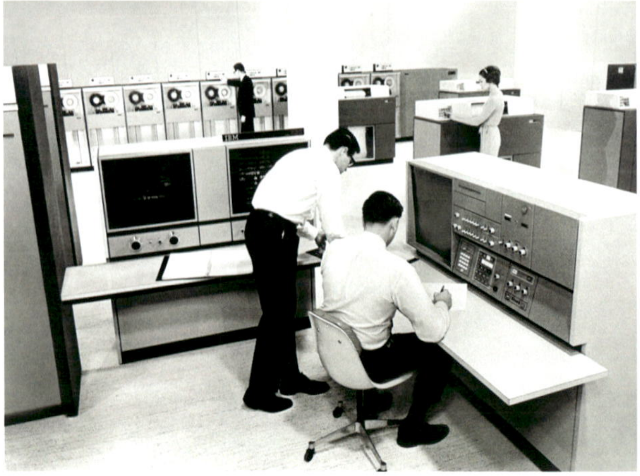


Images courtesy of
IBM Corporate Archives

**Opposite**

*IBM 360/85 (Landscape Proposal)*,
2006 (details)
Maquette
56 x 81 x 36 cm

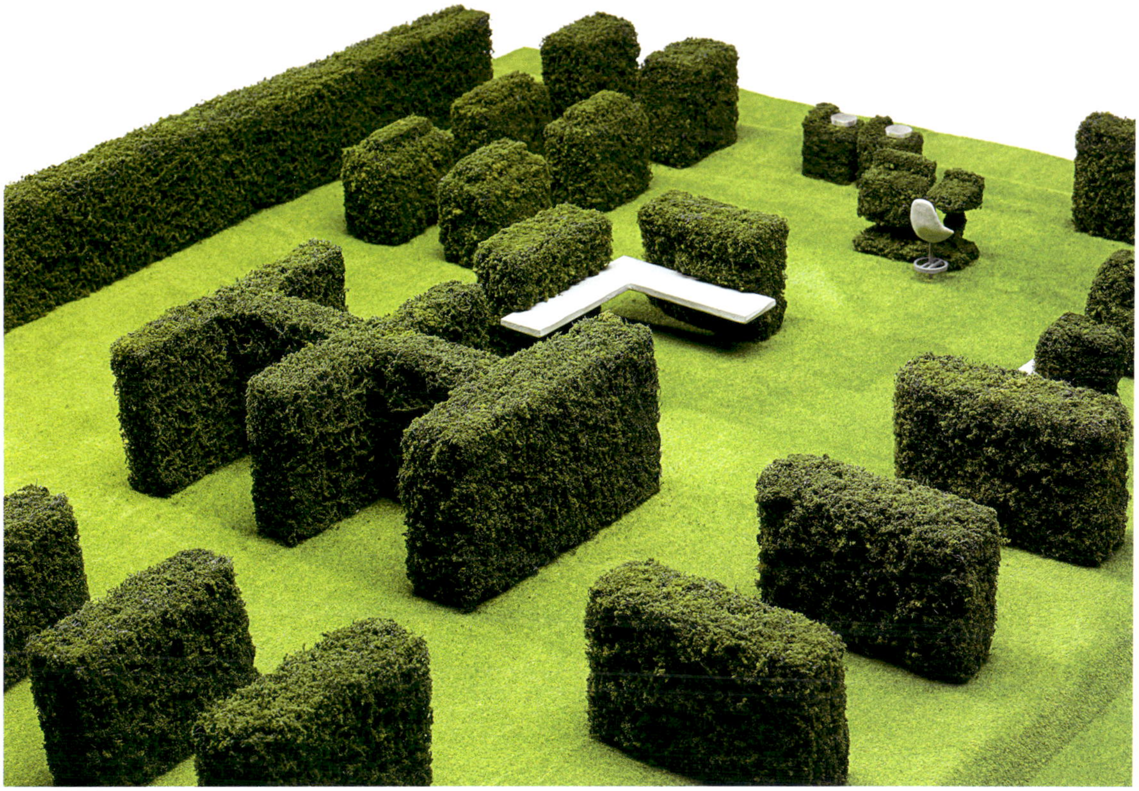

*IBM 360/85* is a proposal for a corporate green space. The form of the IBM 360, the first mainframe computer, would be reproduced in topiary outdoors at 1:1 scale. Worktables and magnetic storage disks would be cast in concrete or polished steel to be integrated with the topiary. While bearing some similarity to the maze-like compositions of aristocratic European gardens, the work embodies the IBM 360's now outdated, spatial language in corporate and computation topologies, as well as interior design.

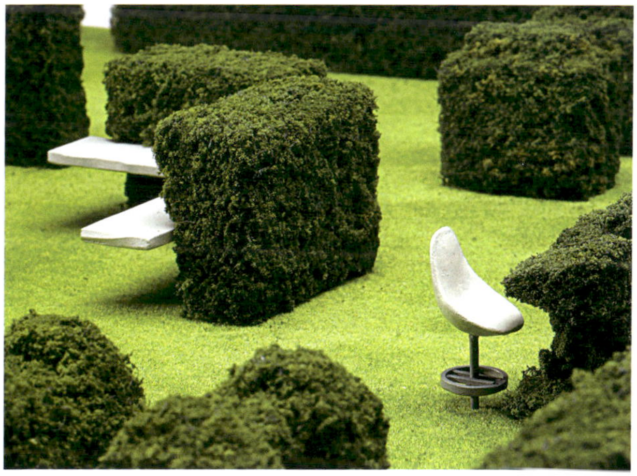

*IBM 360 Panel 65* and *IBM 360 Panel 40* (following page) are 1:1 scale translations of control panels that were a prominent feature of IBM's iconic mainframe computer system in the 1960s. Containing indicator lights, numerical displays, switches and an "emergency pull-stop," these panels were primarily used by technicians who serviced the machines. Designed according to strict principals of intelligibility and ergonomics, these works simultaneously speak to Formalist principles of composition and Minimalist sensibilities of rationalization and seriality.

**Opposite**

*IBM 360 Panel 65*, 2009
Milled and folded aluminum
and custom wall mounts
74 x 92 x 22 cm

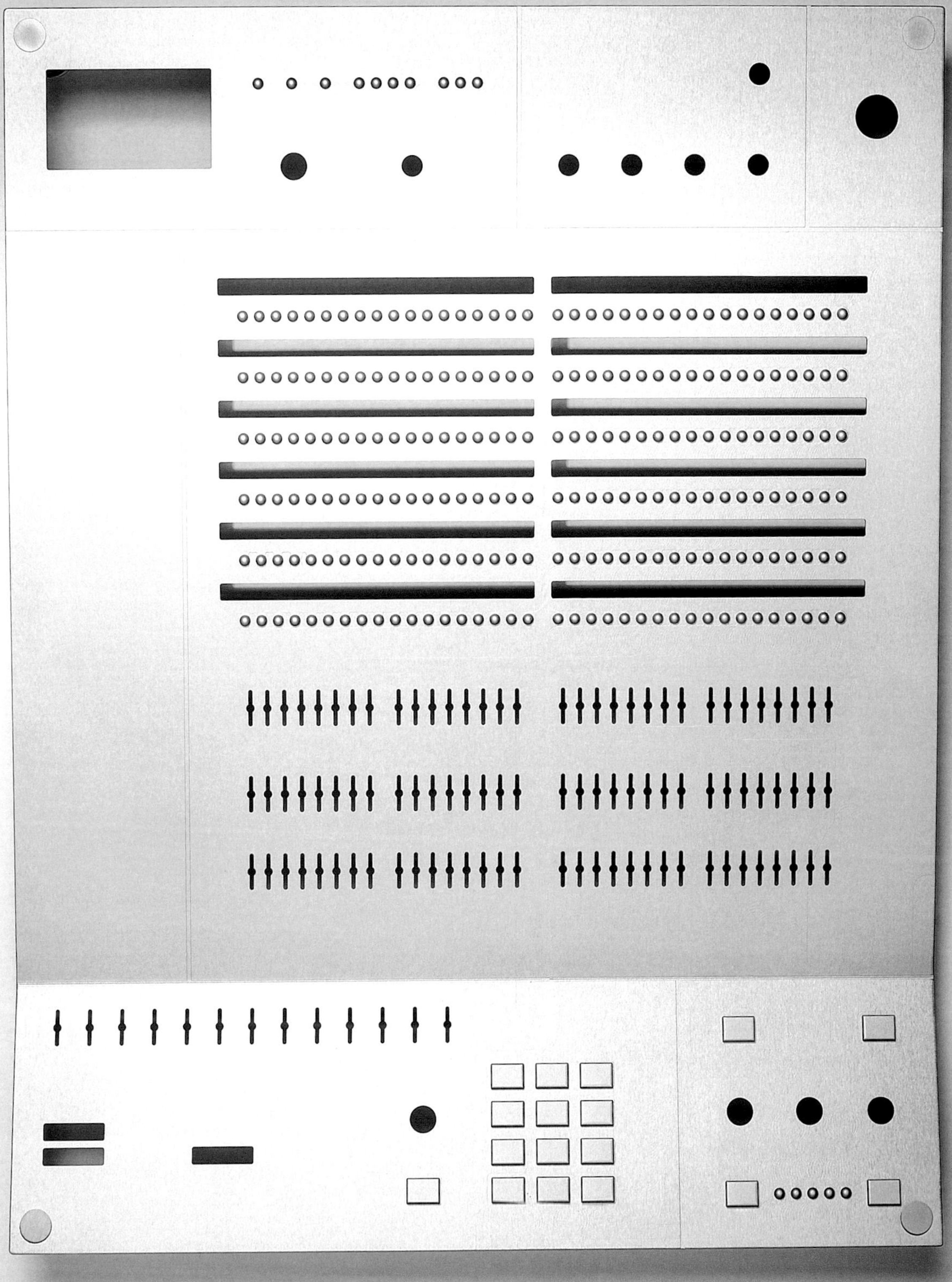

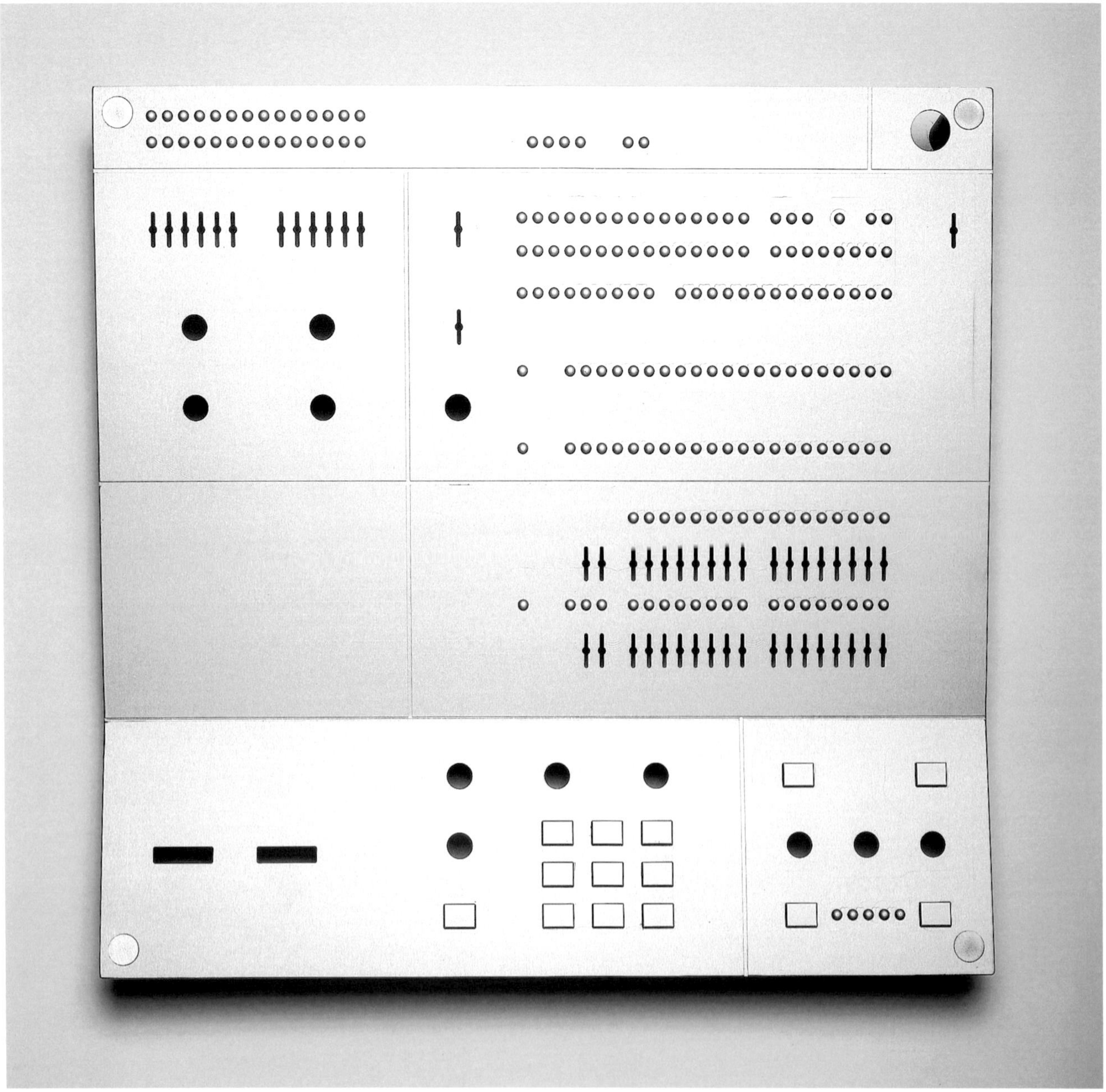

*IBM 360 Panel 40*, 2009
Milled and folded aluminum
and custom wall mounts
71 x 69 x 20 cm

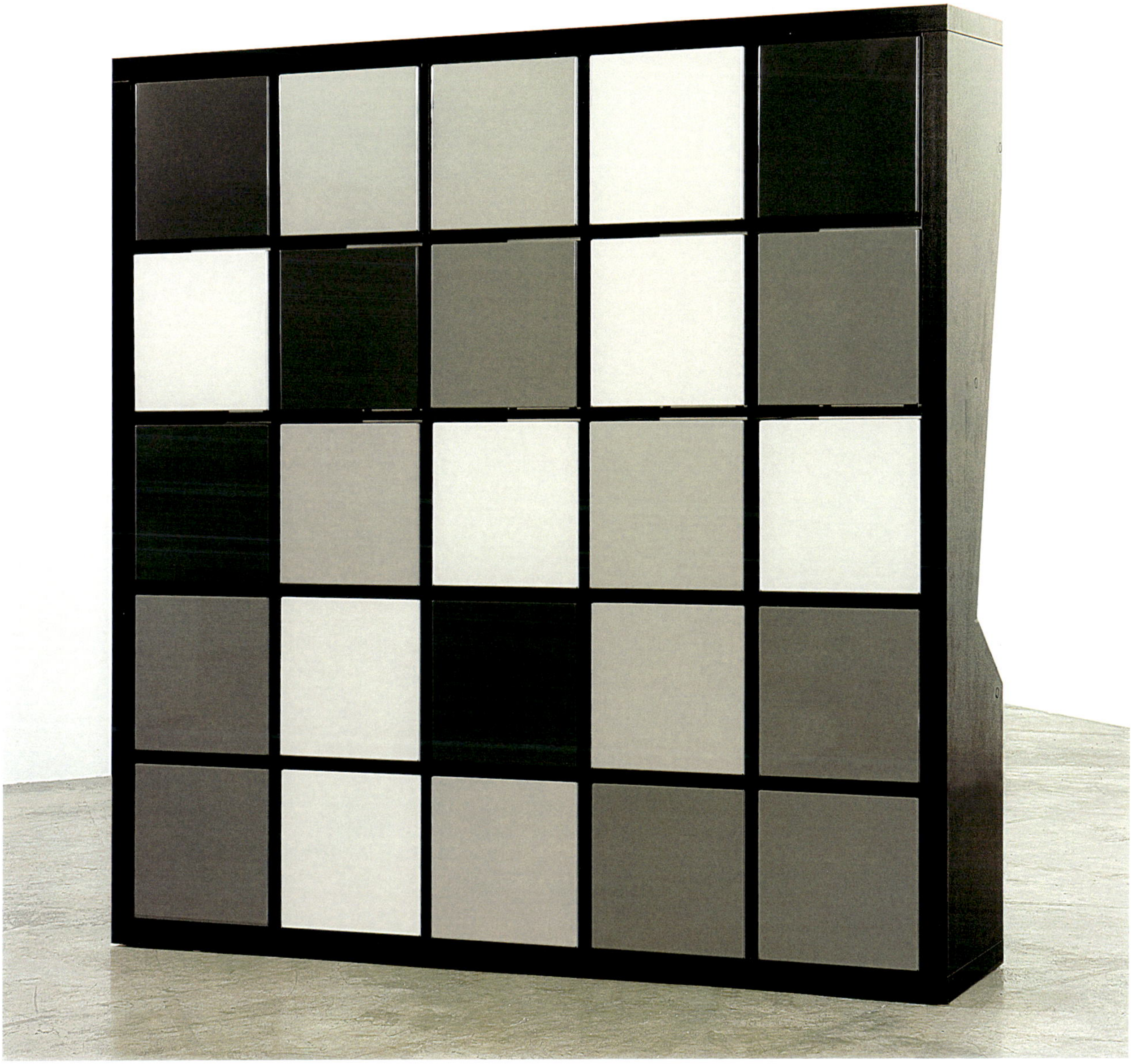

*Brave New Waves*, 2010
Powder coated aluminum enclosures,
milled IKEA and rubber bumpers
185 x 185 x 41 cm

**Opposite**

*Brave New Waves*, 2010
Powder coated aluminum enclosures,
milled IKEA and rubber bumpers
185 x 185 x 41 cm

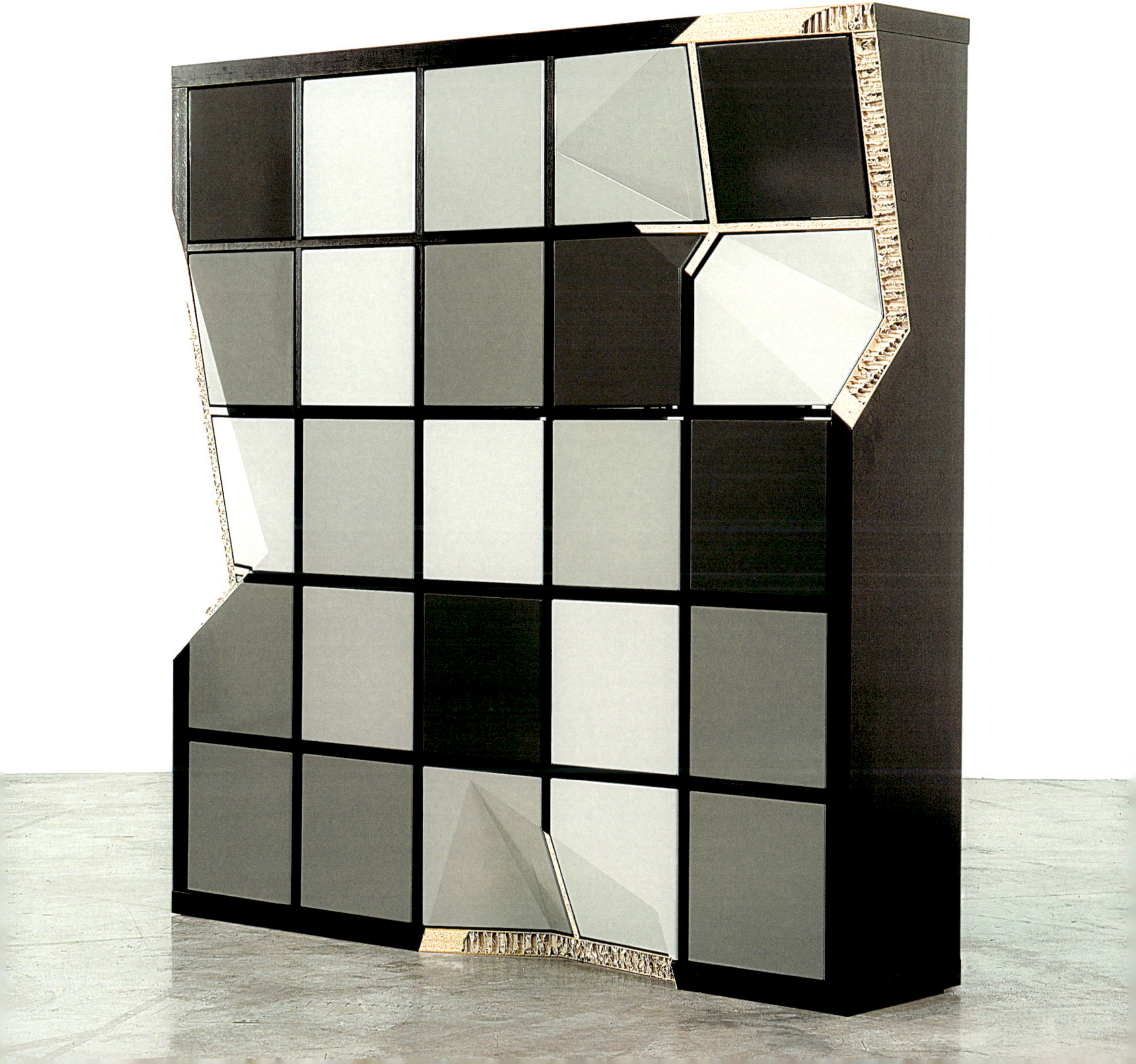

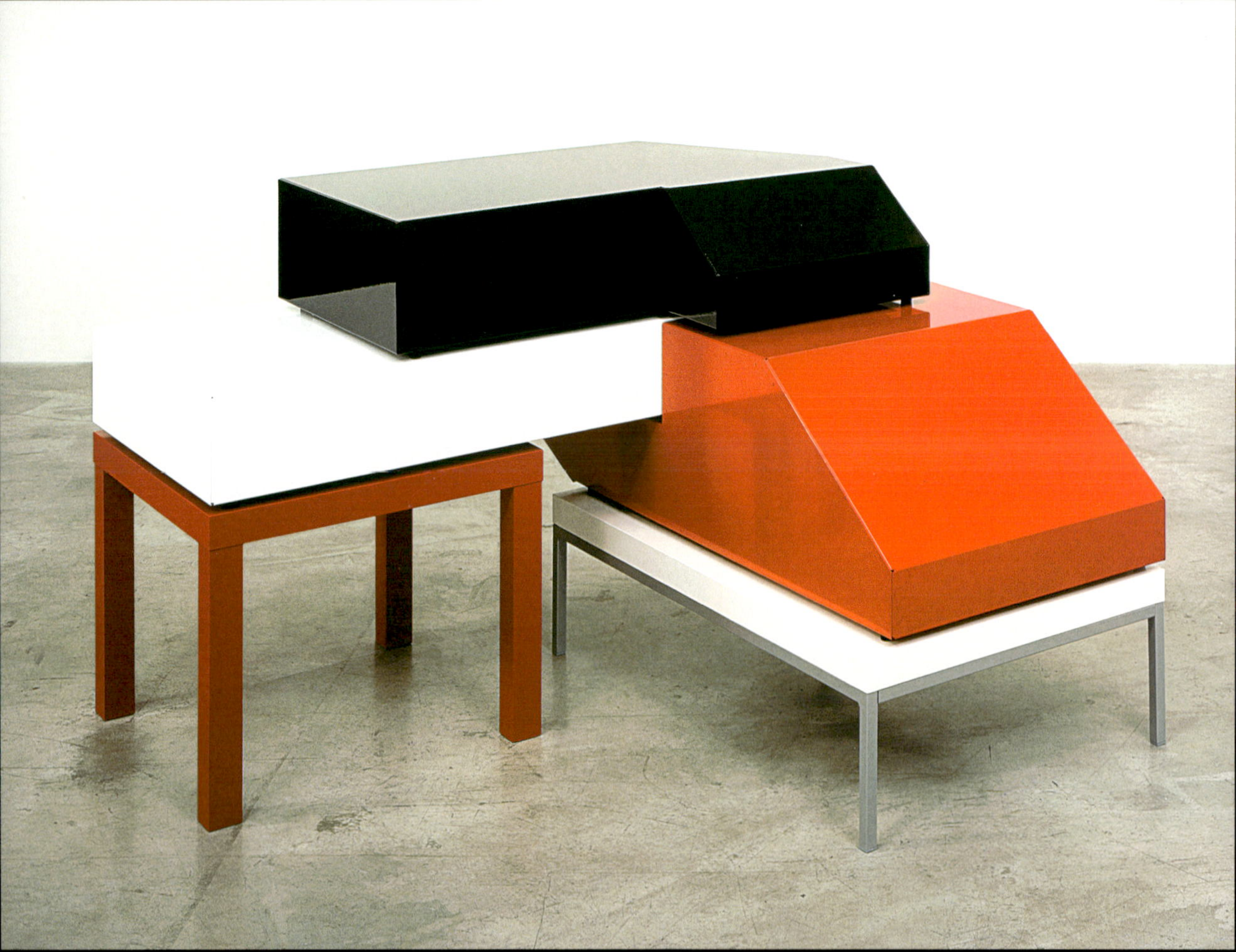

*Arthur*, 2008
Powder coated aluminum enclosures,
IKEA and rubber bumpers
96 x 102 x 72 cm

# The Museum or Landfill

## Walking Through *Boole* and *Beta Boole*

*Most power centers [malls] are risky propositions, as category killers [big-box stores] and discounters battle amongst themselves in submarket-by-submarket survival contests. The only sure thing is that owners will be challenged to re-lease empty boxes abandoned by the losers.*

*Emerging Trends in Real Estate*, 2002[1]

*A standard product, better than most art.*
...
*License against style, good for one week.*

Barrett Watten, from the poem "Direct Address" in *Conduit*, 1988

We might begin our discussion at the atomic level, with the pointed distinction between the ready-made and the custom-made forming the highly abbreviated vocabulary of this sculptural language. Such a vocabulary, grounded in the "infra-ordinary"[2] elements of contemporary built space, strongly invites a psychogeographic reading. This reading cannot proceed without difficulty, however, as the very ubiquity of the work's constituent elements is itself a barrier to locating the spaces to which they might belong, or for which they might stand as models. There is, happily, a localizable point of entry in the immediately recognizable IKEA furniture forming the microcosm of the exhaustive spatial combinatorics on display. These tables, step stools, bookshelves and desks have been configured in an unwitting parody of Constantin Brancusi's—at one time thoughtful but by now merely rustic—integrated pedestals. In this role, they offer themselves as support for a variety of machine- or laser-cut aluminum components finished in a glossy medicinal coating of industrial paint.

On the surface, it is easy to overlook the paradox of a highly specific brand name product adopting the role of a neutral support, but with a little probing this first of many spatial paradoxes embodied in the work reveals itself. We can imagine that in substitute for the IKEA furniture nearly any other artifacts would be aromatic with complex layers of historically-conditioned meaning, much as Daniel Young and Christian Giroux's previous sculptures have been. Instead, the aesthetic of the non-aesthetic is once again resurrected; in this case in the form of what might be technically defined as the anti-competition readymade, to accurately apply a term from neo-classical economics. In this way the very particularity of these readymades, almost accidentally, exposes the banal and yet remarkable domination of our everyday spaces by low costs and predatory pricing. In this sense it is not only the quaint, workman-like and aleatoric eccentricities of a Duchampian readymade that have been dispensed with, force-retired from the most competitive markets by the triumphant neo-liberal logistics of flat packing and tax shelters, but everything else as well. Whether vernacular, functionalist or distinctively stylized, anything with a price deviating from the most affordable is now potentially singled out for appreciation, carrying the premium of a Surrealist *objet trouvé*. As domestic space is infinitely sub-divided at the whim of a struggling middle-class unselfconsciously driven to preserve any remaining material traces of its past within increasingly limited spaces, it is now rare to find an object not partaking of some forceful attraction to one or another facet of an urban interior. As eclecticism replaces snobbism, the pathetic group of objects which somehow do not make the cut—as ironic totem, melancholy medium of heritage, object of pity, or marker of authenticity—are quietly consigned to the realm of thrift, or evaporated unceremoniously, as in Geoffrey Farmer's procedural work *A Pale Fire Freedom Machine* (2005), in which Toronto's Power Plant Contemporary Art Gallery was filled with miraculously ordinary chairs and tables, that were slowly emptied into the floating incinerator of a curvaceous Modernist fireplace. The obverse of this reality is revealed in contrasting Young and Giroux's *Boole* (2008) and *Beta Boole* (2010) with the work that was perhaps the inspiration for *A Pale Fire*, Kippenberger's *The Happy End of Franz Kafka's 'Amerika'* (1994), where each piece of furniture, often without being iconic, cheerfully asserts its own distinction as a virtual artwork seamless with Kippenberger's own creations. It is between these two poles, of distinction and anonymity, that our economic order has neutralized the radicality, uncannyness, the *ostranenie* of "objective chance." What was provocative becomes merely evocative. Certainly, if the dominant players in the marketplace change, or as other artists continue to appropriate identical materials, IKEA designs may also begin to glow with an aura of their own, though it is difficult to imagine their rebirth in the form of anything other than garbage. For the moment, in the absence of a casually or unconsciously invoked canon of IKEA-inspired artworks, these artifacts remain the only available props of a mostly proletarian and lower-middleclass encounter, in the big-box store, at the home-office, cheap hotel, in the corner of an institution, junked on the curb, or found already present in a new apartment.

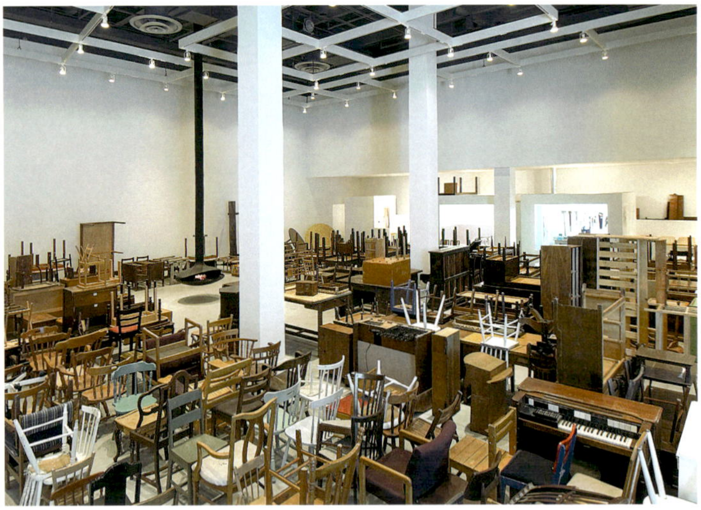

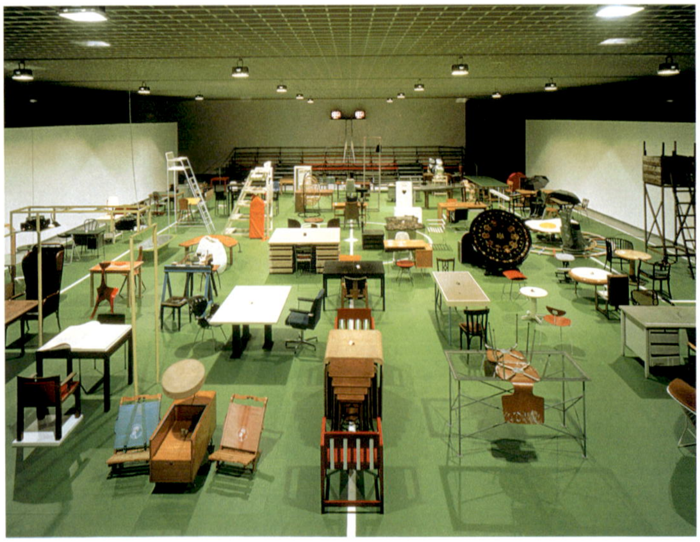

The furniture's belonging in these discrete locations is only accentuated by its being brought forcefully together with the custom-made elements in Young and Giroux's work. The sealed surfaces of those components, exhibiting only minimal traces of construction or assembly, suggest not an alienated form of labour, so much as a, for most people, inaccessible type of highly specialized production for which there is only an unclear set of images. Indeed the digital interfaces that were likely used to render these forms for manufacture are more easily visualized than the environment and machines that finally must have produced them. As a result they appear as near virtual objects, blinking in and out of existence, identical with their conception, though only in a commonplace fashion remote from idealization. In the case of *Brave New Waves* (2010), this is particularly apparent. Colorless boxes fold into exact congruence with the diagonal cuts placed at odds with the shelving's regular grid. These interruptions of the surface expose what is hidden beneath IKEA's slick plastic lamination; its mysterious substance is revealed to be corrugated cardboard, exposed in the manner of computer rendered cut away diagrams found in trade magazine ads. We might wonder if this is *real* cardboard. Our intuition that artificiality is multi-layered, and that nested within second nature are tertiary and quaternary nature, is here confirmed.

Given that, wherever we may be, we are inevitably oriented by our increasingly delimited urban landscape it is difficult to resist the temptation to view *Boole* and *Beta Boole* as contemporary ruins; to enter them via the allegorical road signage of capital vs. consumer, expansive development vs. increasing middle-class poverty; to stand among them as though they were the remnants of a failed franchise, or HO scale "greyfields," the empty malls and big-box stores of recent vintage. There is a certain unease to these works that is not instantly felt. Perhaps it is that the custom-made components, in seemingly violently imposing their own technique of production on the truncated IKEA supports, force them to give up the secret of their shoddy construction; perhaps it is that the found must adapt to the designed in a curious reversal of roles that reinforces a formal hierarchy whereby the furniture is made more homely and familiar even as its opposite is distinguished as an original design. Despite the obvious suggestion involved in sharing a technique, albeit miniaturized to the level of the domestic, the liberatory destruction present in Gordon Matta-Clark's demolitions would thus appear to be a red herring, related more to the poetics of squatting and eviction connected with an earlier phase of urban transformation than to the investigation of the non-spaces proposed by these works.

The consciously composed planes and colour schemes of the custom-made forms in *Kermit* (2008), *Bonsai* (2008) and *The Terrorizers* (2010), in a cursory fashion indifferently associated with Daniel Libeskind, Donald Judd, or friendly Dutch housing projects, are not opposed to the furniture merely in their source of production, but also stylistically. In architecture's own language these are related as "wrapper" and "wrapped," a relationship famously analyzed by Fredric Jameson in the specific exemplar of Canadian architect Frank Gehry's own home.[3] Jameson saw Gehry's corrugated metal and diagonal lines "brutally stamped with the mark and sign of "modern art""[4] as acting on the original pink asbestos-shingled house with hyperreal hallucinatory results. This architectural procedure, which Jameson ironizes as part of a more general Postmodern process of dislocating and fragmenting the ideals of Modernism while simultaneously preserving existing contemporary forms, is well exampled in the artists' home base of Toronto, where Gehry's Art Gallery of Ontario (2008) [AGO], Libeskind's Royal Ontario Museum (2007) [ROM] and Will Alsop's OCAD University (2004) all formulaically apply the "wrapping" procedure to preexisting structures. Twenty years on from Jameson's pilgrimage to the Gehry home, these additions to Toronto's landscape might be better represented as the city's most recent (but quickly tarnishing) bid to stay apace of global rankings in architectural tourism, primarily through the contrivance of the "Bilbao effect." If it is unlikely for us to find in them the vertiginous image of late capitalism rendering hyperreal a hallucinatory past with a well defined exoskeleton of Postmodern materials, these landmarks are correspondingly easy to see as offering a calculatedly distinctive surface without risking transformation of the interior, or of the building playing host. This is particularly true in the case of both the AGO and the ROM, where the original spaces erased or hidden by an addition were unappreciated Modernist designs in their own right. Even where these sculptures most visibly resemble the signature forms of Toronto's spectacular architecture, their topology is turned inside out. The two elements of their composition interpenetrate and

**Opposite**

Geoffrey Farmer
*A Pale Fire Freedom Machine*, 2005
*Collection of Bob Rennie, Vancouver*

Martin Kippenberger
*The Happy End of Franz Kafka's "Amerika"*, 1994
*© Estate Martin Kippenberger, Galerie Gisela Capitain, Cologne*

impinge on one-another's space. Since the customized parts in *Boole* and *Beta Boole* fully subsume and yet are bounded by the fresh items of trash that sustain them they are left to exhaustively explore their own concavities in a fashion more characteristic of the logic (both its rigors and its freedoms) of modern spaces and forms than the arbitrarily protruding stilts, flukes and vertices at which they hint.

Thus, allegory is played out somewhat differently in the space of the gallery proper. There it could be reported as an art historical conflict in which territorial lines have been drawn (often simplistically) between artist's deploying techniques of appropriation and recontextualization in the service of institutional critique, on the side of the readymade, and proponents of High Modernism, here most obviously embodied in the custom-made components' plausible ancestry in the "specific objects" of Judd, as already suggested. Oddly enough, it is through figuration that the aluminum constructions, when conceived as either maquettes or as full-scale models, cross this demarcation. The resemblance of the boxes assembled on the rickety table in *Bonsai* to external hard drives or shipping containers (brought neatly into contact with their flat packed cargo), or the resemblance of the green cells stacked on the side table in *Kermit* to an inadequate office filing system, render banal Minimalism's rhetoric of Modernist concentration, rigor and transparency. Though they seem prototypical, one is still tempted to handle these works, to test if they will not slide open to reveal filing cards, circuit boards or paper clips.These can not be the first artworks to suggest, that in relation to the structure of everyday life, Minimalist aesthetics obediently adapt to nearly any purpose, be they those of global transit, bureaucratic information systems, or simple bourgeois fastidiousness. Self-contained, understated and clearly circumscribed, Minimalism is more vulnerable to these appropriations than the arresting or imposing, confrontational or dynamic forms of other strains of Modernism.

The complex relations between these prominent bi-ways of art history are well-modeled and tested in *Boole* and *Beta Boole*. The diagonal forms of *Arthur* (2008), presumably named after another Canadian architect, Arthur Erickson (whose Brutalist buildings are well represented in Toronto), spill from one table to another, according to what is, when compared to the static composition of the majority of these works, an animated if not expressive geometry. Looking at *Arthur* we can't help but see, in part at the invitation of its colour pallette, an atavistic form struggling to defy gravity and reconnect to the radical history of the Russian avant-garde, to leave the pedestal and totally integrate itself into the display space, like an encaged specimen of El Lissitzky's *Proun Room* (1923). Even after excavating the diverse locations and antecedents within the work, the readymades retain a powerful leveling effect. They serve to expose, literally through physical contact and symbolically through comparison, certain types of Minimalist and High Modernist sculpture to the concrete geography of everyday life at its most commercially abject. They suggest a *détournement* of their valuation when set autonomously against the gallery floor.

Given the thoroughness of the artists' program, the work's critical impact remains highly circumscribed, implicit and not didactic. This is particularly clear in the case of *Mao* (2008), which comes perilously close to the type of high-design object that a critical practice might attempt to expose, and which a High Modernism might seek to distinguish from itself if not transcend. Encapsulated in the meeting of the white table with this variation on the Minimalist cube is the type of over-designed retail space from which one departs, leaving behind the atmosphere of exclusivity and tastefulness conferred by the displays, having purchased the same junk available everywhere else. Appropriately, this is the only work in which the custom-made has traded the role of support with the readymade. From this vantage it is easy to imagine design students coming away from these shows armed with a full portfolio of inspiration. Equally, one can imagine the artists themselves expanding the editioning of the

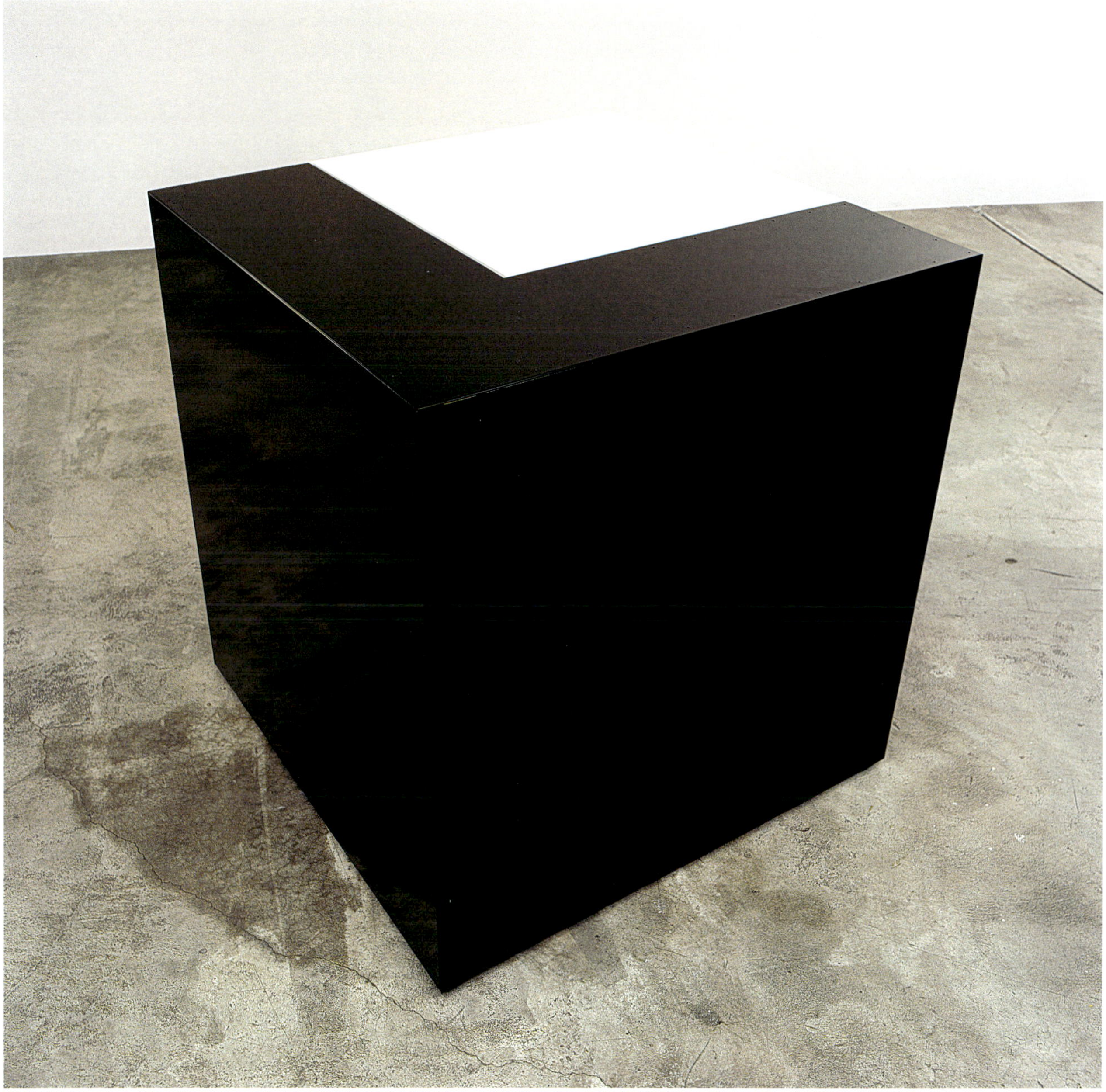

*Mao,* 2008
Powder coated aluminum enclosure,
IKEA and rubber bumpers
80 x 80 x 80 cm

works in order to make them available to home decorators. Insofar as the IKEA furniture aspires to an iconic evocation of High Modernist design, and insofar as Minimalist aesthetics might strip away the already minimized signature Modernist styles in the pursuit of structural primitives, the two types of opposed objects will touch if not intersect at their outer limits. We are forced to conclude the obvious while seeing it afresh, that both are commodities, though of distinctly different life cycle. Outside of this stalemate, planning, the utopian potential of a fortuitous meeting of the readymade and the custom-made, is only present in speculative form. Under our own economic order the destination of these components when separated, in either landfill or a museum, serves as a diagnostic map of our urban geography and the gallery system.

## JESSE HUISKEN

*Jesse Huisken is a writer, artist and bookseller based in Toronto. He is currently working on an experimental prose exploration of Toronto's urban geography.*

Daniel Young and Christian Giroux's *Boole* (2008) and *Beta Boole* (2010) exhibitions were originally presented in Toronto at Diaz Contemporary.

### Notes

1. Report sponsored by Pricewaterhouse Coopers and Lend Lease Real Estate Investments "Emerging Trends in Real Estate," (2002 & 2003). Cited in: Mitchell, Stacy. *Big Box Swindle: The True Cost of Mega-Retailers and the Fight for America's Independent Business.* Boston: Beacon Press (2006).

2. Paul Virilio claims the term as his and George Perec's, in a psychogeographic repurposing of Duchamp's concept of the "infra-slim." Duchamp was quoted as having "chose on purpose the word slim which is a word with human, affective connotations, and is not an exact laboratory measure. The sound or the music which corduroy trousers [...] make when one moves, is pertinent to infra-slim. The hollow in the paper between the front and back of a thin sheet of paper [...]" (Duchamp 1973, p 194). Virilio defines the "infra-ordinary" as "what we do when we do nothing, what we hear when we hear nothing, what happens when nothing happens" (AA Files, p 15). He further describes it as an alternative to the "traditional urban geography (cadastral survey, social classes, concentration, density & other phenomena)" (ibid).

3. Gehry Residence (1978), located in Santa Monica, California

4. Jameson 1991, p 112.

### Works Cited


Duchamp, Marcel. *Salt Seller: The Writings of Marcel Duchamp (Marchand Du Sel)*. New York: Oxford University Press (1973).

Jameson, Fredric. *Postmodernism, or, the Cultural Logic of Late Capitalism*. Durham: Duke University Press (1991).

Rappolt, Mark. Ed. *AA Files 45/46: Georges Perec & Paris*. London: Architectural Association Files (2002).

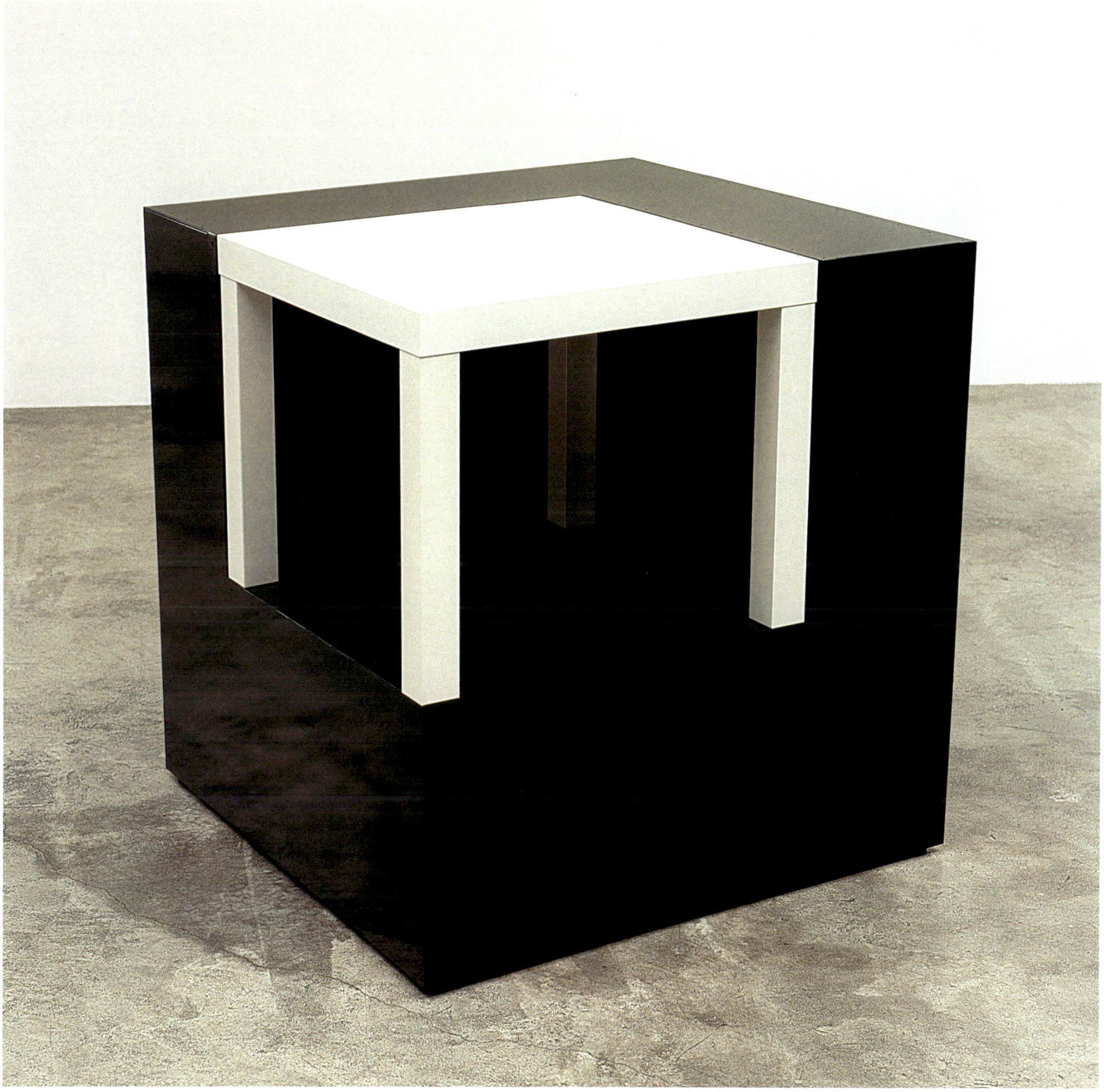

*Mao*, 2008
Powder coated aluminum enclosure,
IKEA and rubber bumpers
80 x 80 x 80 cm

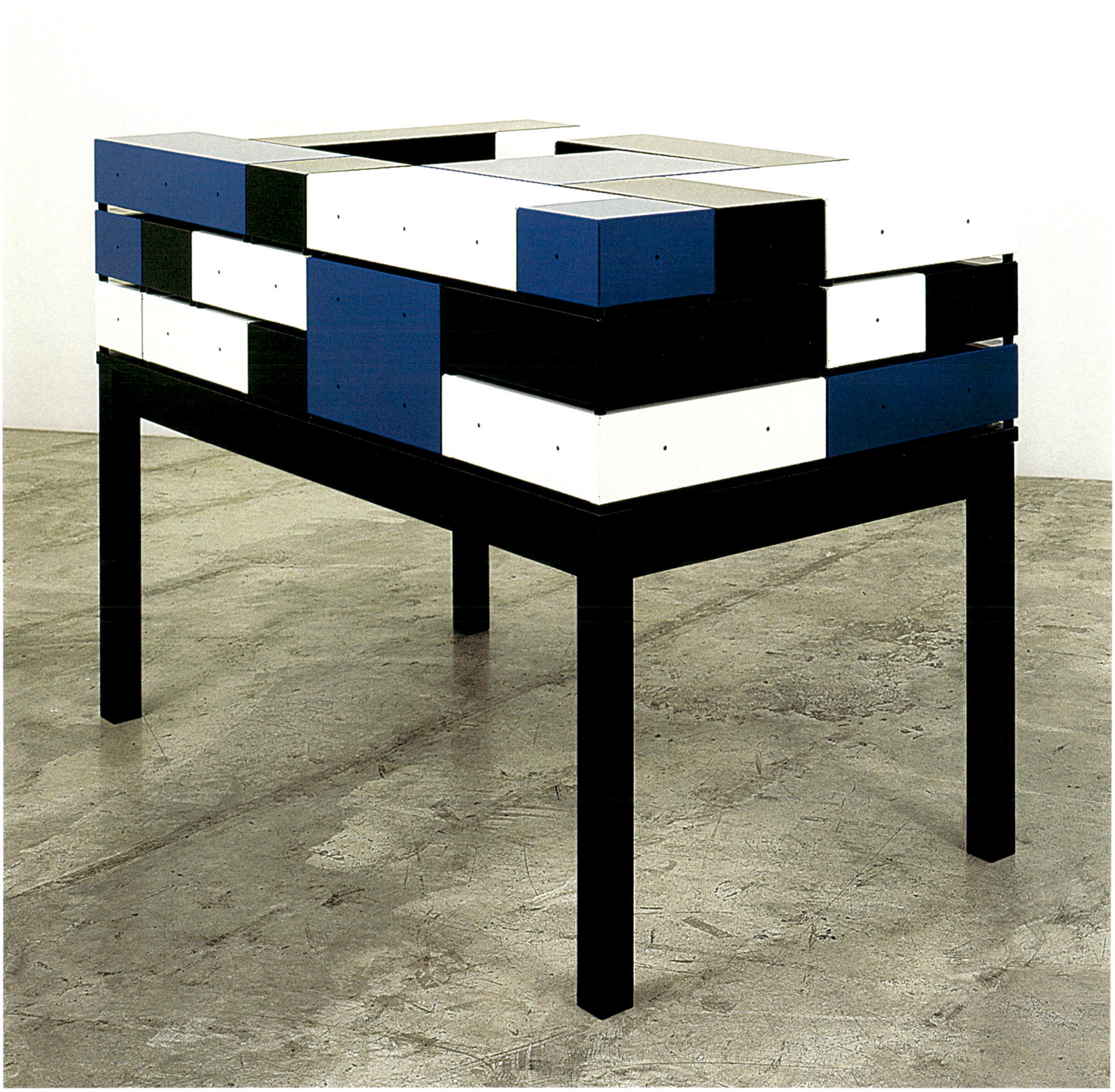

*Bonsai*, 2008
Powder coated aluminum enclosures,
milled IKEA and rubber bumpers
94 x 175 x 132 cm

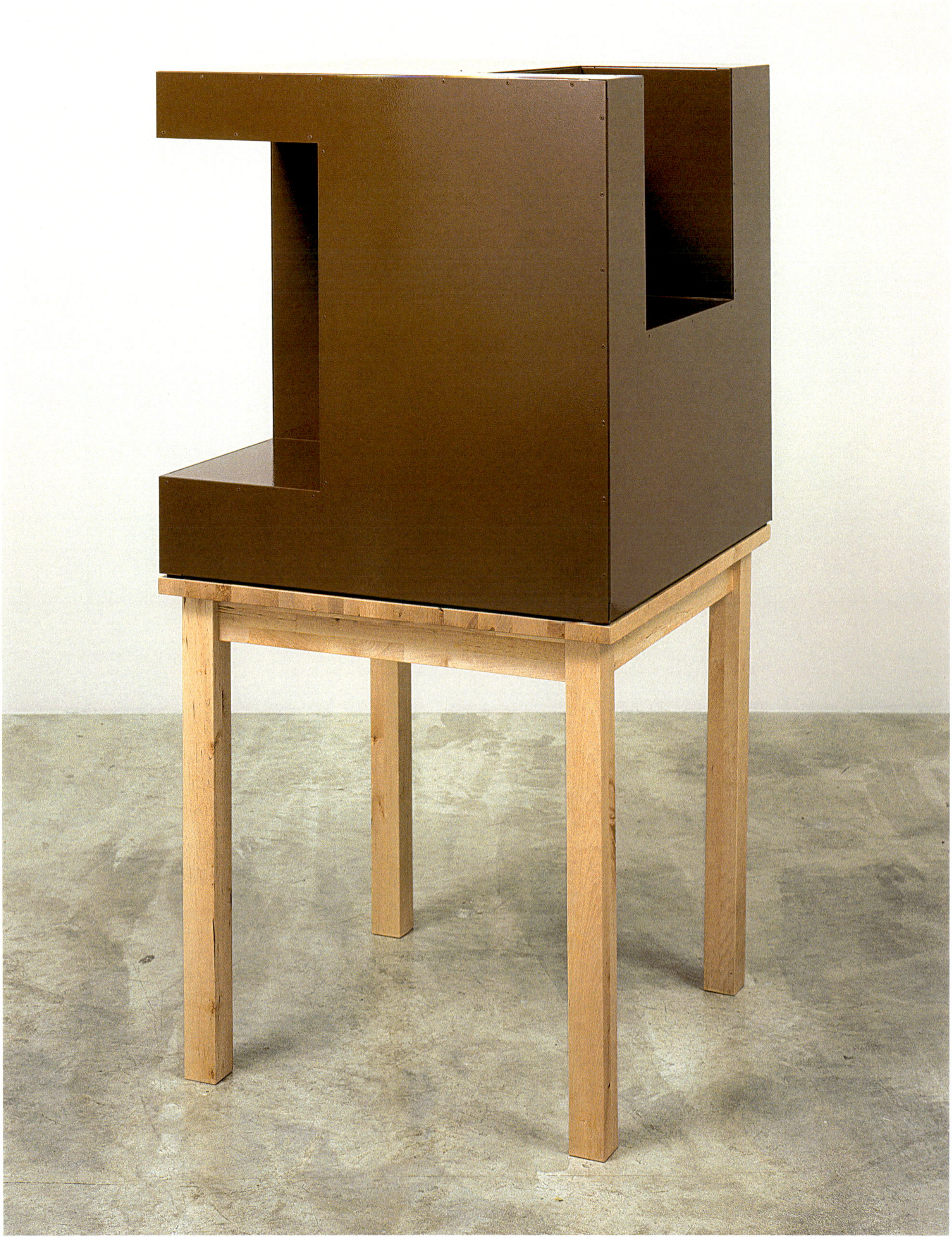

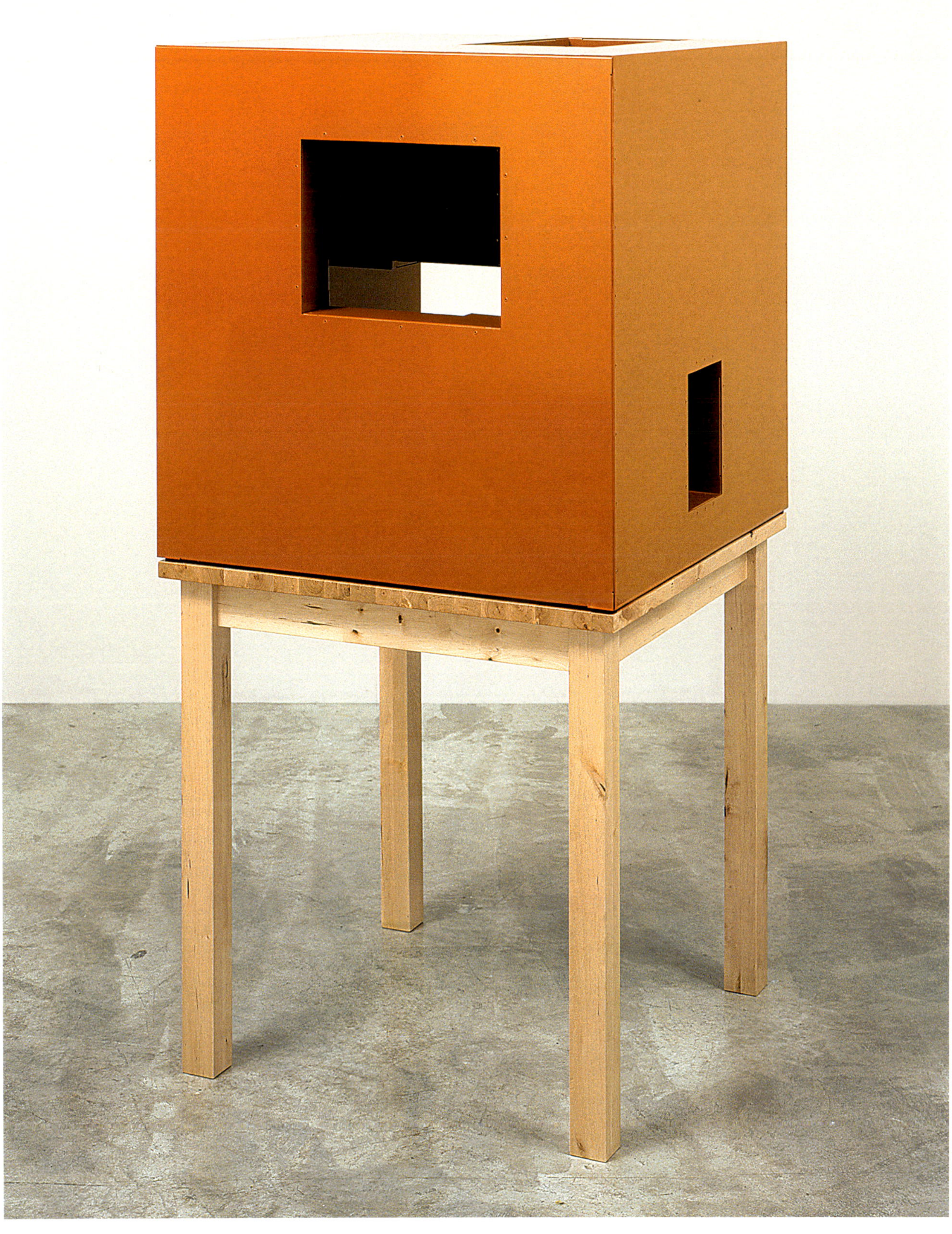

**Previous**

*Umbria*, 2008
Powder coated aluminum enclosure,
milled IKEA and rubber bumpers
145 x 74 x 74 cm

*Sienna*, 2008
Powder coated aluminum enclosure,
milled IKEA and rubber bumpers
145 x 74 x 74 cm

**Opposite**

*Kermit*, 2008
Powder coated aluminum enclosures,
milled IKEA and rubber bumpers
55 x 55 x 82 cm
*Collection of David and Yvonne Fleck*

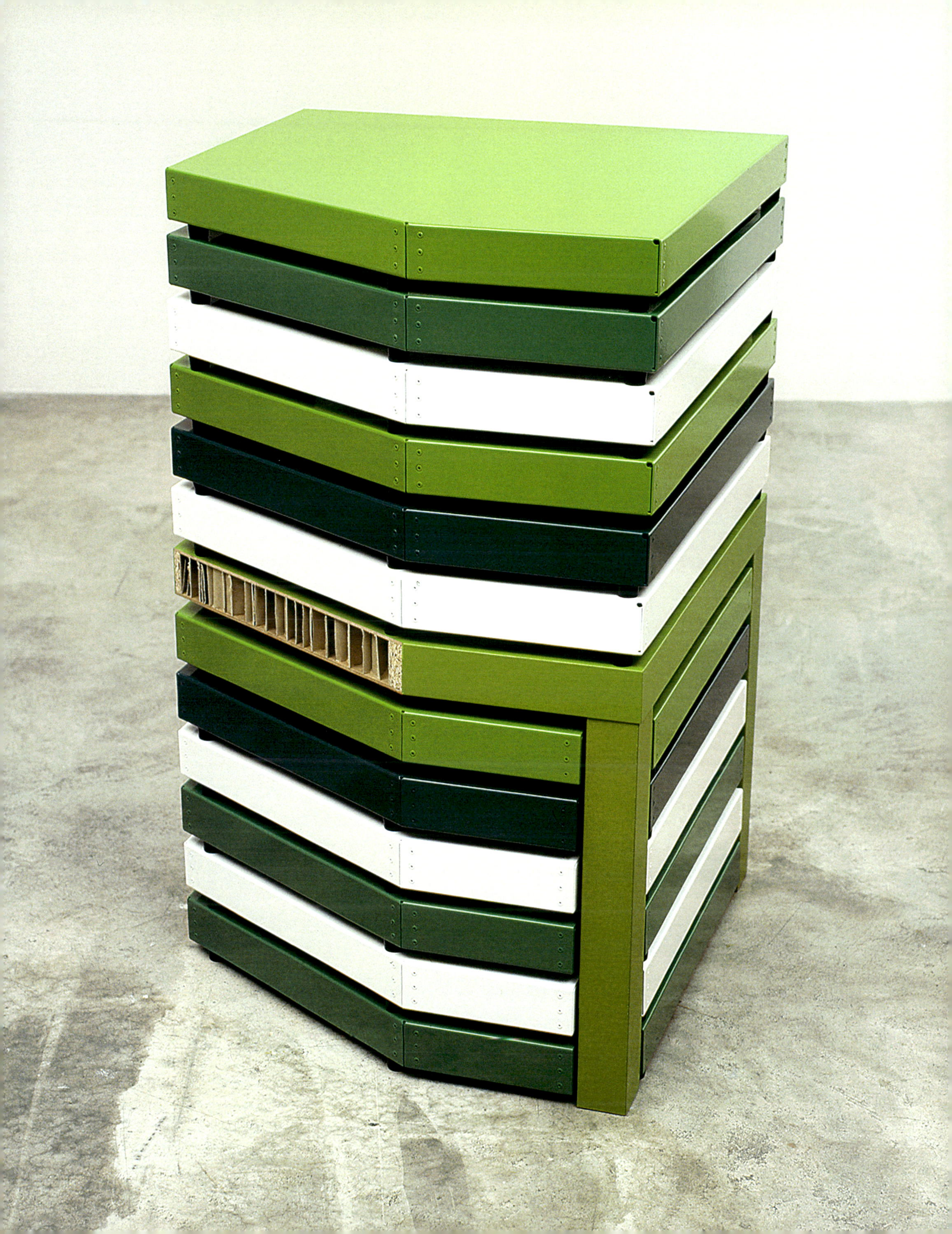

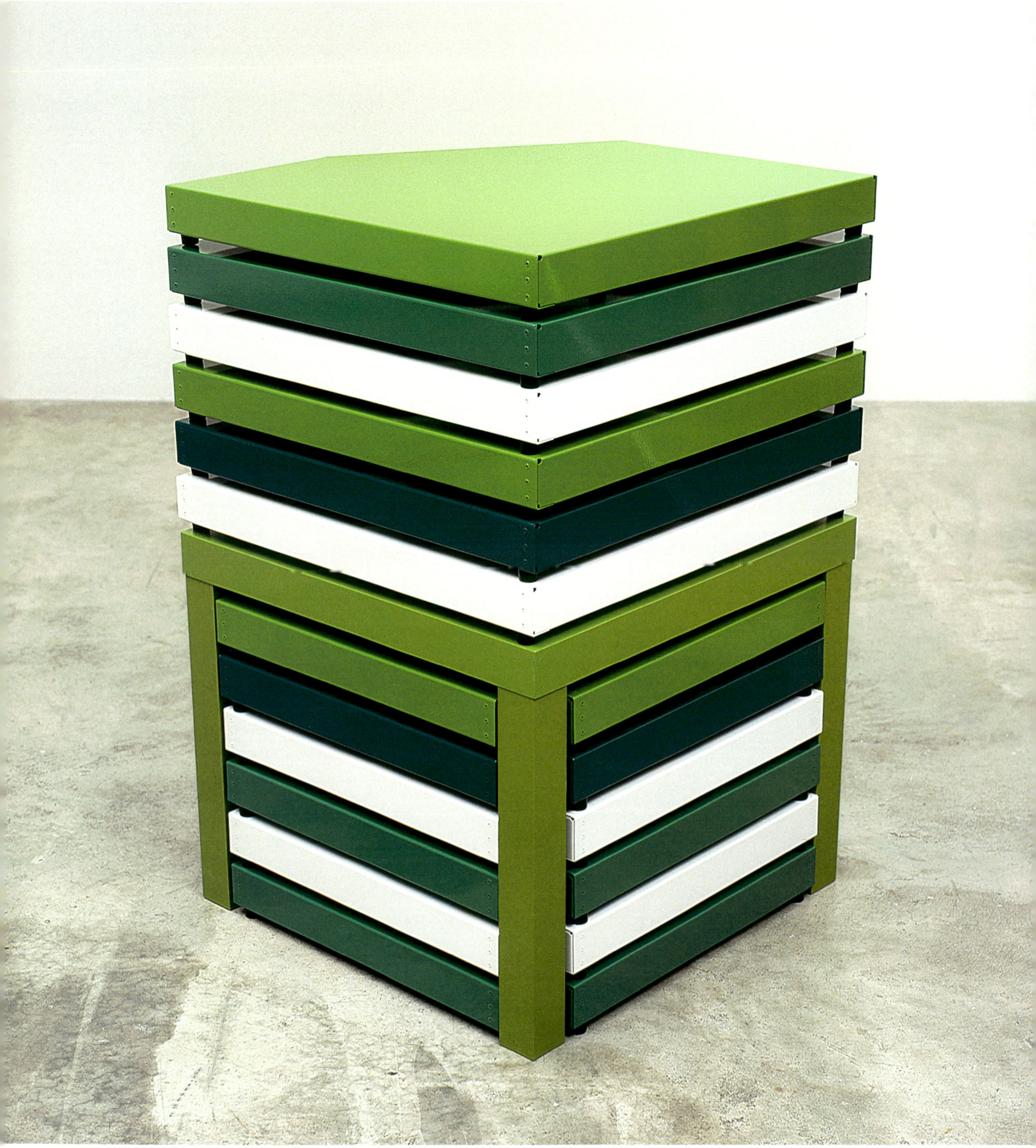

**Opposite**

*Kermit*, 2000
Powder coated aluminum enclosures,
milled IKEA and rubber bumpers
55 x 55 x 82 cm

*Collection of David and Yvonne Fleck*

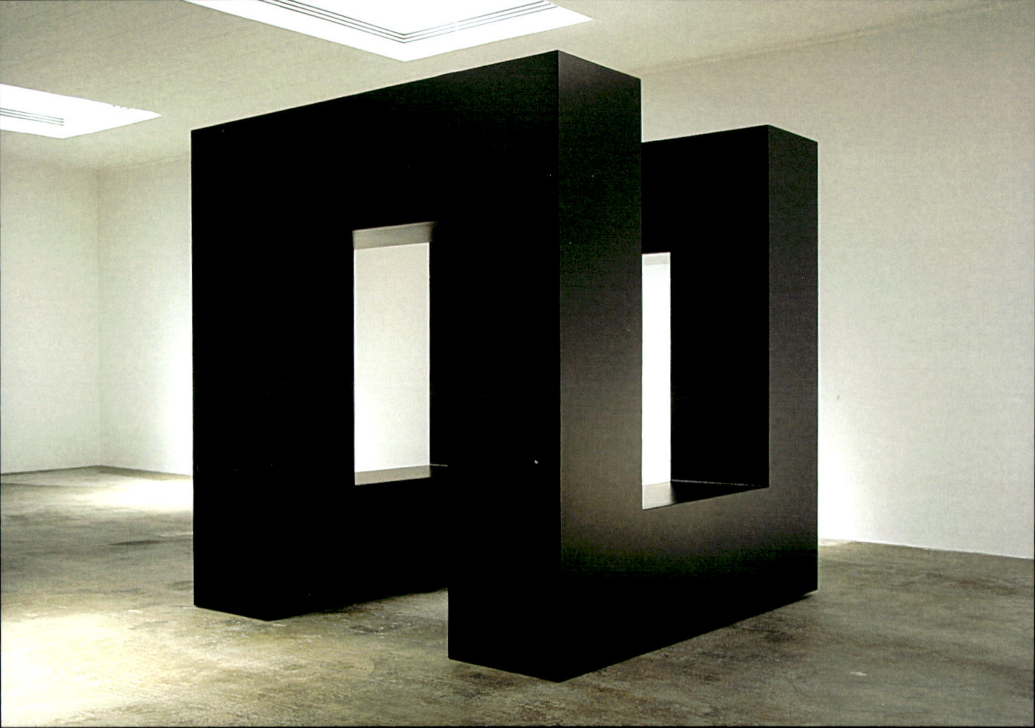

Tony Smith
*We Lost*, 1962
*Courtesy of Matthew Marks Gallery, New York*

# Are All Oppositions Equal?

Daniel Young and Christian Giroux have collaborated since 2002 on sculptures, public artworks and film installations. In sculpture, they rework the abstract forms associated with Modernism, using consumer products and items related to design and industrial production techniques. Their film pieces arise out of their investigation of the sculptural forms that underlie the built environment. In their art, they introduce sequences of antinomic yet complementary notions (systemic/arbitrary; present/past; ugly/beautiful; specific/generic; signed/anonymous; regionalism/internationalism) which generate a dialectic that shifts a reading of their works from one that is strictly phenomenological—related to their roots in formalism—to one with a political content, related to the utopian dimension of the Modernist project, particularly in architecture.

The contrasting or complementarity of opposites can often lead to a simplistic, even reductive, highlighting of dualities. Indeed, more often than not it involves clichés like presence/absence or here/elsewhere, observations that, as appropriate as they may be to the work under discussion, offer little insight. However, generally speaking, the exhibiting of works of art resembles a certain dialectical model: one work sheds light on aspects of another, and vice versa, thereby setting up a dialogue which, in the best instance, fades into the background in order to better illuminate the issues that drive an entire approach. This is especially true since an exhibition, in essence, remains a dialogue between objects (the works) and subjects (the visitors).

This bias against an oppositional structure as model is all the more misplaced when applied to the work of artists Daniel Young and Christian Giroux as a whole and, more specifically, the presentation of two of their works at the Musée d'art contemporain de Montréal in early 2011 in which the diaglogue between a sculpture and a film takes the built environment as its subject. *Mr. Smith* (2011) is a near-monumental sculpture whose form is derived from the compositional grid employed by American artist Tony Smith (1912-80) in his sculptures in the 1960s. The film *Every Building, or Site, that a Building Permit has been Issued for a New Building in Toronto in 2006* (2008) consists of a series of static shots that, as the title states, document every building or site for which a permit was issued in Toronto in 2006. It has a running time of about thirteen minutes, or eight seconds per shot of each of the 115 sites documented.[1]

The juxtaposition and confronting of these two different works yield a certain perspective: here, sculpture is to the exhibition gallery what a building represents to the city. A new set of binary relations is thus added to those we have already proposed: sculpture/architecture, object/space, site/non-site.

Without copying any specific piece by Tony Smith, the artists have created, in *Mr. Smith*, a system of triangular surfaces and wooden struts connected to one another with a system of cast aluminum joints and assembled according to the space available. In so doing, they have produced a work that gives visual form to the structural logic of Smith's sculptures while also utilizing the non-linear spatial potential of the modular, almost architectural nature of his art.[2] A number of conversations are going on between the different components of this piece—at the very least, between its underlying structure and its final form. The result is a hybrid structure in which a space-frame type of system cohabits with the triangular planes, adding further complexity to the relationship between the spaces (negative) and volumes (positive) of the sculpture. As was noted by Georges Didi-Huberman, Smith's sculpture "can be viewed as a big toy (*Spiel*) allowing a dialectic, visual working of the tragedy of the visible and the invisible, the open and the closed, mass and excavation." Citing *We Lost* (1962-66) as an example, that author sees it as a work "that affirms its mass—a monumental cube—only through the close interplay of the exposed voids, those we can slip into and pass through, and the superimposed voids within the body of the sculpture itself."[3] By making this visual dialectic an integral, internal part of the form that constitutes the sculpture, Young and Giroux multiply the original effect that lies at the heart of Tony Smith's work.

Young and Giroux's re-examination of Tony Smith is in keeping with certain current artistic practices that have a historicizing approach. And indeed, after more than forty years of differentiating and distancing themselves from the Modernist canon, how do these practices broach some of its characteristics without being explicitly reactive to or in line with Modernism? It should be made clear, right off, that, by Modernism, we mean the application of a reductionist style that proposes a dilution of the visual components in order to form a terse aesthetic statement, as well as the subjecting of the form of the built environment to the function performed by its constituent parts (the role of architecture in the organization of capitalist society, the famous "form follows function"). Modernism would thus express a questioning of issues that are both aesthetic (philosophical) and political (ideological).

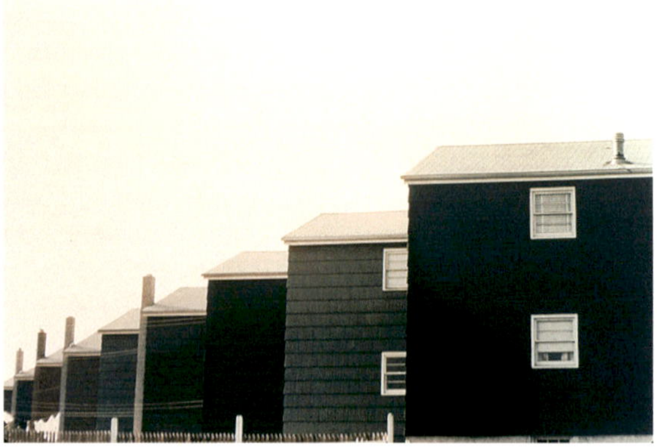

Dan Graham
*Homes for America*, 1966-67 (detail)
*Courtesy of the artist and Marian Goodman Gallery, New York*

Taking non-hierarchical elements from the built landscape (urban, industrial) and subjecting them to an analytical gaze is a strategy that has been employed from the very beginning of Conceptual art, and that offers an experience of the everyday site in comparison with the historicized ("mythologized") site. While Young and Giroux, in formulating the title of their film, may refer to Edward Ruscha (more specifically, his 1966 work *Every Building on the Sunset Strip*[4]), there are numerous examples of this type of representation in images of a (quasi) systemic protocol between the mid-1960s and the late 1970s: Dan Graham (*Homes for America*, 1966-67), Robert Smithson (*A Tour of the Monuments of Passaic New Jersey*, 1967), Jeff Wall (*Landscape Manual*, 1969), Ian Wallace (*Elevator Piece*, 1970) and Bill Vazan (*Yonge Street Walk*, 1969-72), to name only a few. In these works, the objects (often photographic) are the result of more or less predetermined actions, forming a documentary corpus that bears witness to a system which existed for a given period of time, in some random, often urban, space and which carries little symbolic weight.

The film *Every Building, or Site, that a Building Permit has been Issued for a New Building in Toronto in 2006* charts the city of Toronto, not by locating the sites in a defined spatial grid, but rather by setting them within a specific time frame that is actually determined by a bureaucratic procedure: the issuing of permits in the year 2006. The sequence of shots is based on the chronological order in which the permits were issued. Consequently, while this interest in documenting the current state of the vernacular architecture necessarily looks at the

**Opposite**

*Every Building, or Site, that a Building Permit was Issued for a New Building in Toronto in 2006*, 2008 (frame scans)
35mm colour motion picture film (1:1.85), no sound, 13 min looping film installation

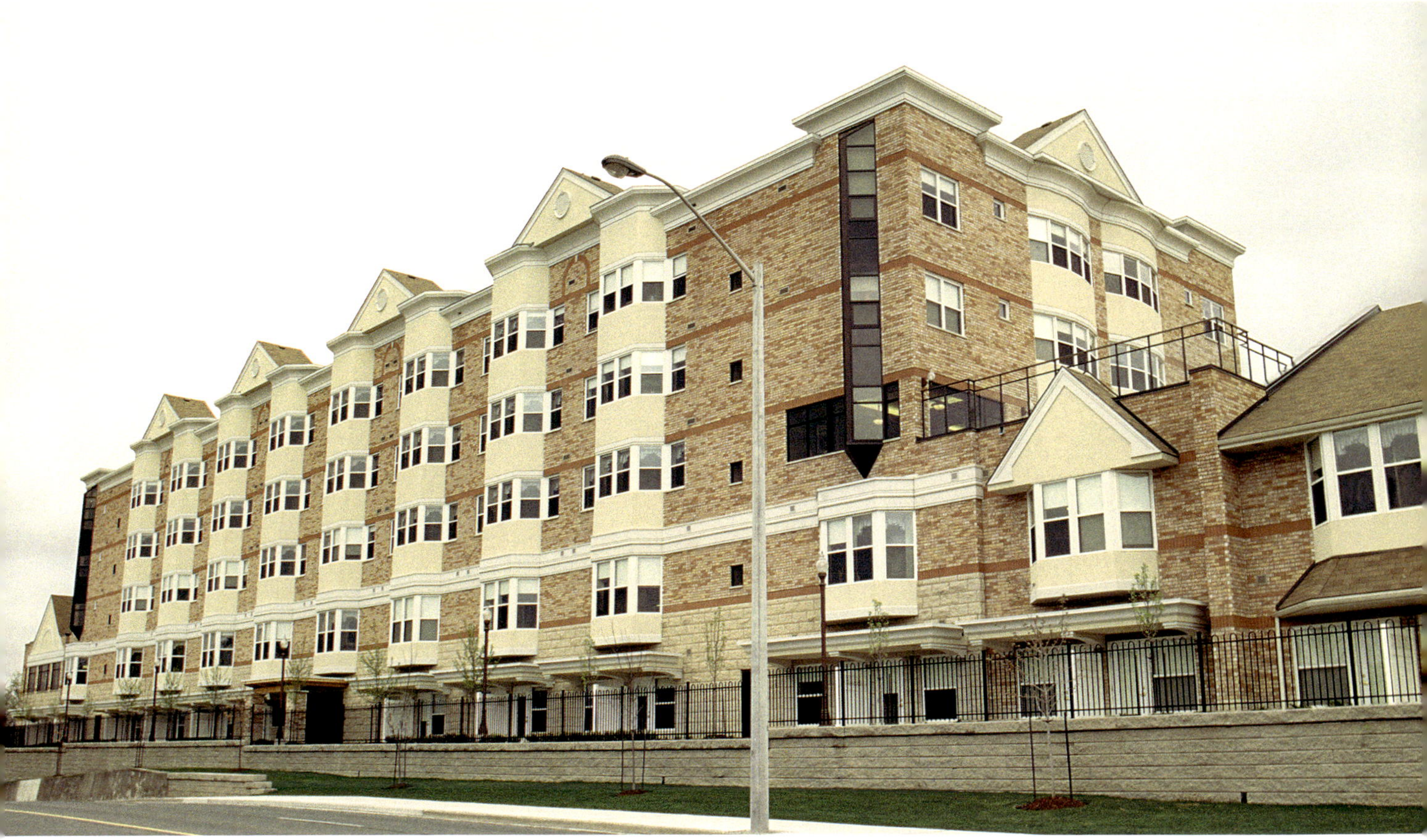

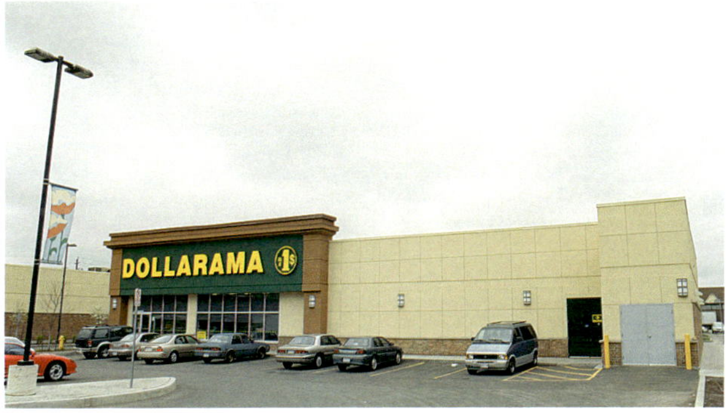
DOLLARAMA

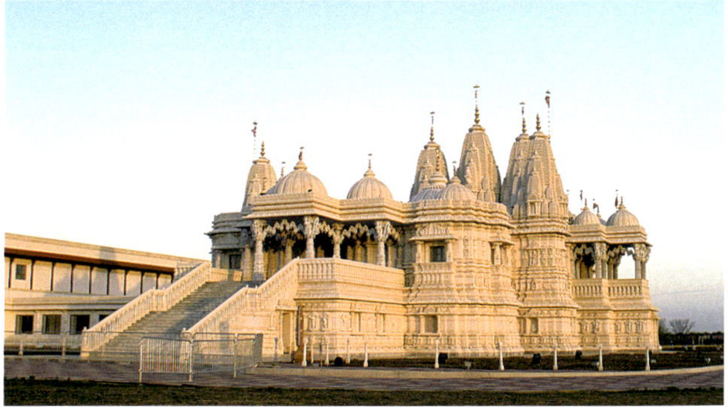

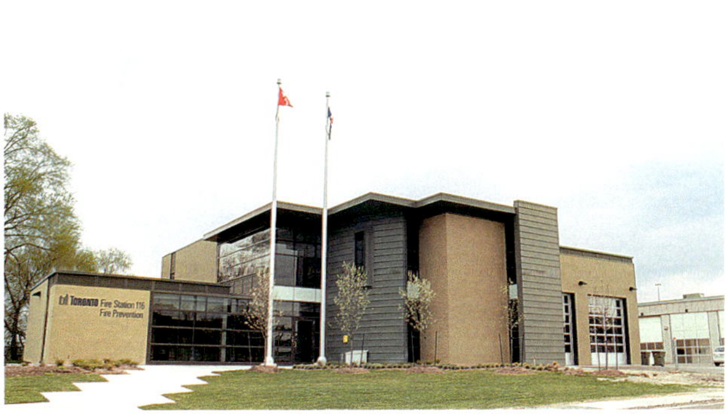
Toronto Fire Station 116
Fire Prevention

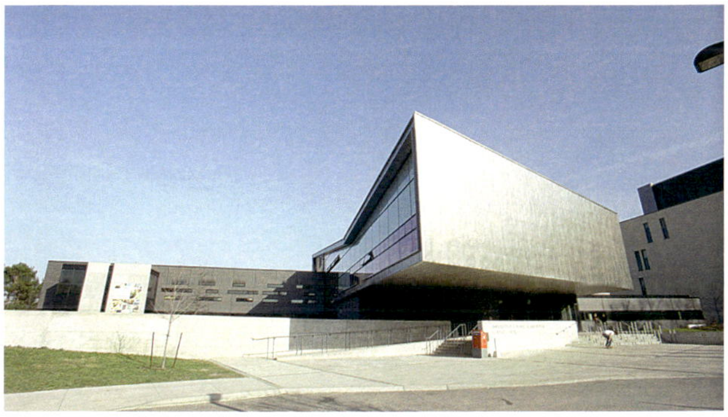

present, it also traces a link (less direct than the reference to Tony Smith) with the conceptual art of the 1970s, evoking practices that tend to combine the systemic (procedure, protocol) with the random (the subjects covered).

We can see Tony Smith as another case of meaningful ambivalence. He belongs to the generation of the Abstract Expressionists yet is also considered a pioneer of Minimalist sculpture. His visionary works foreshadowed the emergence of the resolutely Minimalist art of Donald Judd, Carl Andre and Robert Morris, among others;[5] however, from the generational standpoint, he was no doubt one of the targets of the defenders of Conceptual art who advocated a certain devaluing of the object. And yet, in 1966, Smith wrote a famous piece which appeared in the December issue of *Artforum*—and which complicates the question. Even though this text has been oft-quoted since it was published, I would like to reproduce an extended excerpt here on the limitations of art compared with an experience of the built environment:

> When I was teaching at Cooper Union in the first year or two of the '50s, someone told me how I could get on to the unfinished New Jersey Turnpike. I took three students and drove from somewhere in the Meadows to New Brunswick. It was a dark night and there were no lights or shoulder markers, lines, railings or anything at all except the dark pavement moving through the landscape of the flats, rimmed by hills in the distance, but punctuated by stacks, towers, fumes and colored lights. This drive was a revealing experience. The road and much of the landscape was artificial, and yet it couldn't be called a work of art. On the other hand, it did something for me that art had never done. At first I didn't know what it was, but its effect was to liberate me from many of the views I had had about art. It seemed that there had been a reality there which had not had any expression in art.
>
> The experience on the road was something mapped out but not socially recognized. I thought to myself, it ought to be clear that's the end of art. Most paintings look pretty pictorial after that. There is no way you can frame it, you just have to experience it. Later I discovered some abandoned airstrips in Europe—abandoned works, Surrealist landscapes, something that had nothing to do with any function, created worlds without tradition. Artificial landscape without cultural precedent began to dawn on me. There is a drill ground in Nuremberg, large enough to accommodate two million men. The entire field is enclosed with high embankments and towers. The concrete approach is three 16-inch steps, one above the other, stretching for a mile or so.[6]

In this passage, Smith compares his experience of a semi-industrial landscape with the most basic form that underlies it. He would thus be, in spite of himself perhaps, a forerunner of both the Minimalism of Donald Judd and the Land Art of Robert Smithson.[7] Closer to us here, this excerpt provides a greater understanding of what connects *Mr. Smith* and *Every Building*.... The exhibiting of these two works side by side does more than illustrate a metonymy in which the relationship between object and place becomes a link between sculpture/building and gallery/site. In light of the description of an experience similar to the Industrial Sublime[8]—evinced by Smith in the preceding text—a certain political (ideological) perspective takes shape. Smith paints a striking picture of it by evoking, without dwelling on it, the *Reichsparteitagsgelände* (the site of the Nazis' mass rallies in Nuremberg). In seeing this charged space as nothing more than a monumental, sparsely built open area (cold form), Smith raises reluctantly (and *in absentia*) the question of the ideological import of architecture (hot content). If Young and Giroux, like other artists who carry out systemic inventories, focus intently on the current architectural landscape of Toronto, it is because they are also sensitive to this question. The disarming banality of today's vernacular architecture itself carries meaning. On the one hand, we can see in the buildings they filmed the antithesis of the utopian architecture that was

**Opposite**

*Every Building, or Site, that a building permit was issued for a New Building in Toronto in 2006*, 2008 (installation view)

*Hayes House (Landscape Proposal for a Public Park)*, 2005
Maquette
50 x 76 x 45 cm

characteristic of twentieth-century Modernism. On the other hand, the predictability of the urban landscape they observe leads us to believe that the advent of technocratic urban societies is accompanied by an aesthetic neutrality that tries not to offend anyone. Contemporary urban development seems to follow a logic of popular consensus that imposes a banality on the built environment. This is certainly taken up in the language used to describe the evolution of urban development. As Lucy Lippard has noted: "From 'slum clearance' to 'urban renewal' to 'redevelopment,' the nomenclature of efforts to re-engineer cities has gone from blatantly imperialistic to pseudo-optimistic to a neutrality that almost admits past mistakes."[9] The clean aesthetic desired to bring out the function of a structure's components (elimination of ornamentation, purity of line, emphasis on materials, simple geometry, open spaces) would imply avoiding any ideological reference in designing a new vernacular, in spite of the many attempts to apply this ideology in the latter half of the twentieth century. (We only have to look at how Brutalism and housing projects have become synonymous with alienation in the collective imagination.)

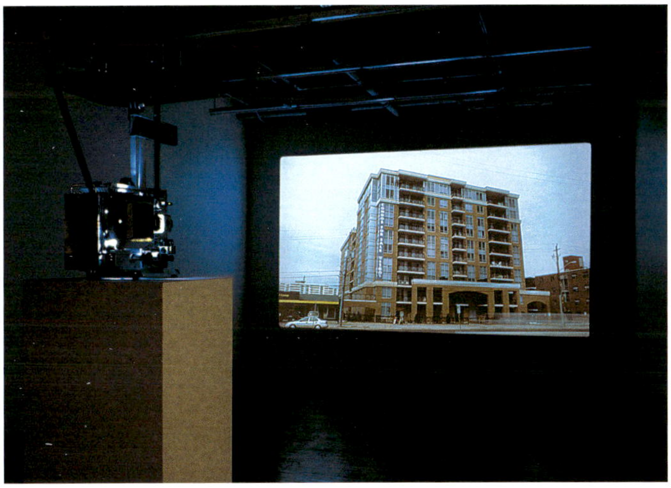

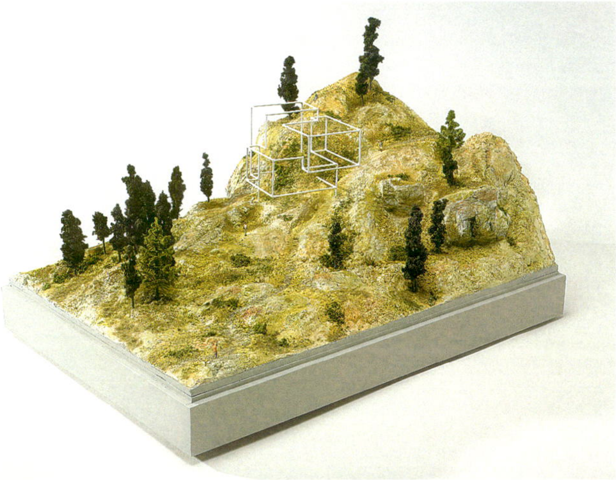

Just as Modernism seems to waver between the technocratic efficiency of urban planning (Le Corbusier, Mies van der Rohe) and the apparent political disengagement of Formalism (Clement Greenberg, Post-painterly abstraction), the contemporary world imposes its own politico-ideological readings that are distinct from those put forward by the champions of Postmodernism (Neo-Geo, Pictures Generation), which developed reactively in the 1980s. Young and Giroux go back to the Foucauldian perspective associated with Modernism's architectural utopias,[10] in response to the major issues that arise out of the globalized capitalist economy. Their choices in terms of style (abstraction) and production techniques and materials (aluminum and plywood, made in factories and woodworking shops from maquettes created with 3-D modelling software) form the core of their practice.

The artists thus challenge the received notions of Modernism in general, but wonder, above all, how today's architecture and sculpture, as close or far as they may be from Modernist issues, continue to be formed by an ideology at the same time as it is informed by them. For Young and Giroux, it is a matter of establishing a dialogue about the form contemporary society continues to give itself: they observe the evolution of this form over time (the more, or less, distant past) and space (more, or less, nearby places) in order to better draw from it sources of inspiration and subjects to explore.

One source of this way of doing things may be found in a change in attitude perceptible at the centre of the emergence of Postmodernism. Robert Venturi, Denise Scott Brown and Steven Izenour comment on it in their groundbreaking study that came out in the early 1970s, *Learning from Las Vegas*: "Learning from the existing landscape is a way of being revolutionary for an architect. Not the obvious way, which is to tear down Paris and to begin again, as Le Corbusier suggested in the 1920s, but another, more tolerant way: that is to question how we look at things."[11] Since then, what matters goes beyond any distinctions between present and past; ugly and beautiful; specific and generic; signed and anonymous; regionalism and internationalism; and, above all, function and form. In their scope, the works of Young and Giroux endeavour to move away from their status as signs; they become paradoxical objects that sustain both a retrospective and a prospective gaze while also keeping very present this dual perspective.


### MARK LANCTÔT

*Mark Lanctôt is a curator at the Musée d'art contemporain de Montréal.*



This essay accompanied the exhibition *Young & Giroux*, presented at the Musée d'art contemporain de Montréal from February 3 to April 25, 2011.


#### Notes

1. Previous presentations of this work included 107 buildings and sites. Eight more sites were added to complete the film.

2. Tony Smith also maintained an architectural practice.

3. Georges Didi-Huberman, *Ce que nous voyons, ce qui nous regarde* (Paris: Éditions de Minuit, Collection "Critique," 1992) pp 77-78.

4. On the connection between *Every Building...* and conceptual art, see Peggy Gale, "Assembling the Givens," *Prefix Photo* 19 (May 2009), pp 20-33.

5. Smith sets himself apart from the Minimalists in stating: ""The main difference in approach, as I understand it is that the minimalists are aiming at certain results, while my work is the product of a variety of processes which are not governed by conscious goals."." Quoted by R. Neu in the brochure accompanying the exhibition *Tony Smith*, Museum of Modern Art, New York, 1968, reprinted (in French translation) in Jean Pierre Criqui, "Trictrac pour Tony Smith," *Artstudio* 6 (Fall 1987), p 39.

6. Samuel J. Wagstaff Jr., "Talking with Tony Smith," *Artforum* (December 1966), p 19.

7. This "bridge" between Minimalism and built environment is probably expressed most clearly in Dan Graham's *Homes For America*. As Scott Watson puts it: "By means of photographs of tract houses that had an uncanny resemblance to Judd's rows of boxes, Graham, in *Homes for America* (1966), implicated the minimalist row of boxes in a more general economy." Scott Watson, "Discovering the Defeatured Landscape," in Stan Douglas, ed., *Vancouver Anthology: The Institutional Politics of Art* (Vancouver: Talon Books, 1991), p 252.

8. For more on the link between the industrialization of the United States and the emergence of Industrial Sublime, see David E. Nye, *American Technological Sublime* (Cambridge, Mass.: MIT Press, 1996), in particular Chapter 5, p 109: "The Factory: From Pastoral Mill to Industrial Sublime," which contains the following: "At first, steam-driven factories were subsumed within the pastoral tradition, but by the end of the [19th] century, they were seen as sublime precisely because they were intensely unnatural."

9. Lucy R. Lippard, *The Lure of the Local: Senses of Place in a Multicentered Society* (New York: The New Press, 1998), pp 204-05. See also Camilo José Vergera, *The New American Ghetto* (New Brunswick, N.J.: Rutgers University Press, 1995).

10. By Foucauldian, I mean more specifically Gilles Deleuze's reading of Foucault's theory of the Panopticon: "The abstract formula for Panopticonism is no longer 'to see without being seen' but to impose a particular conduct on a particular human multiplicity." Gilles Deleuze, *Foucault*, trans. S. Hand (Minneapolis: University of Minnesota Press, 1988), p 34; originally published in French as *Foucault*, 1986. This, of course, is articulated best through the production of space that is architecture and urban planning.

11. Robert Venturi, Denise Scott Brown and Steven Izenour, *Learning from Las Vegas: The Forgotten Symbolism of Architectural Form* (Cambridge, Mass.: MIT Press, 1972-77), p 3.

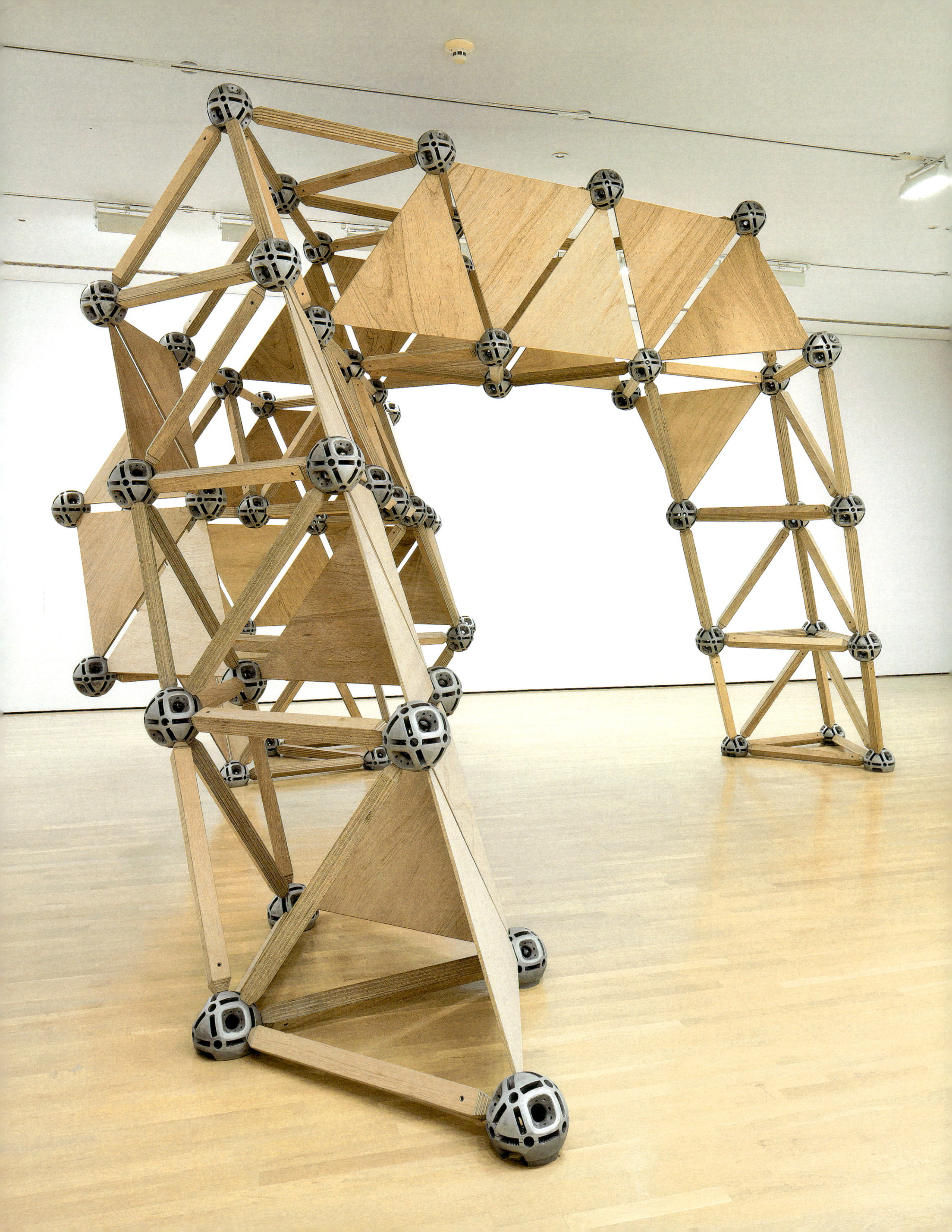

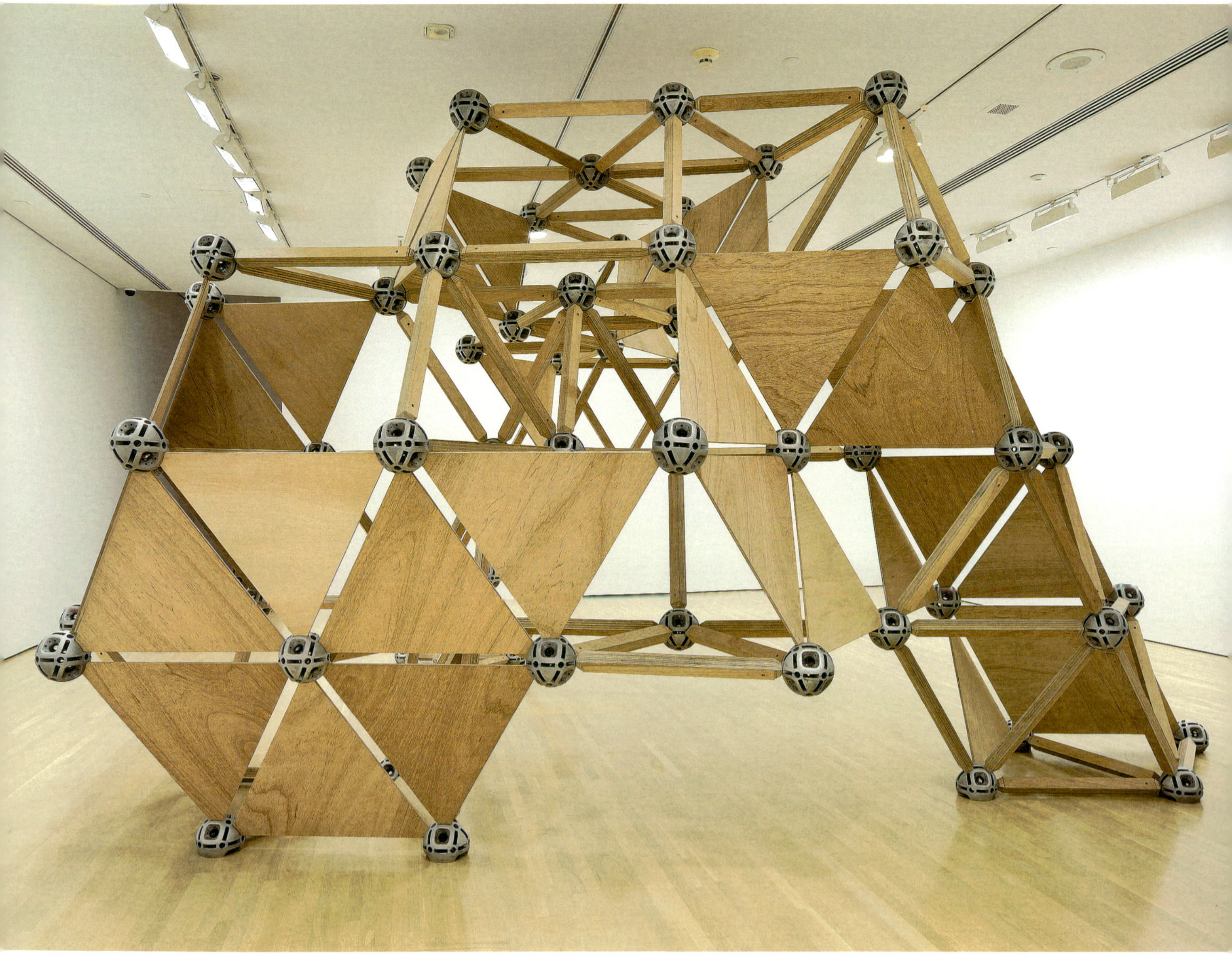

*Mr. Smith*, 2011
Cast and machined aluminum,
plywood and fasteners
Dimensions variable

**Previous**
*Mr. Smith*, 2011

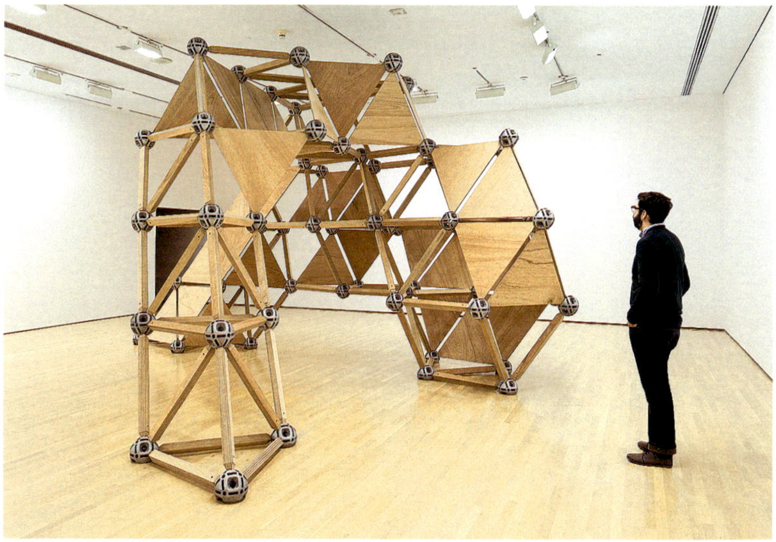

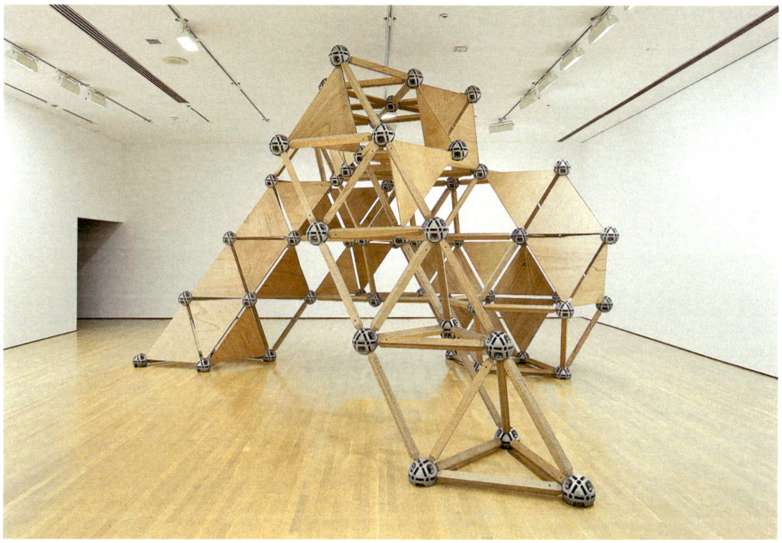

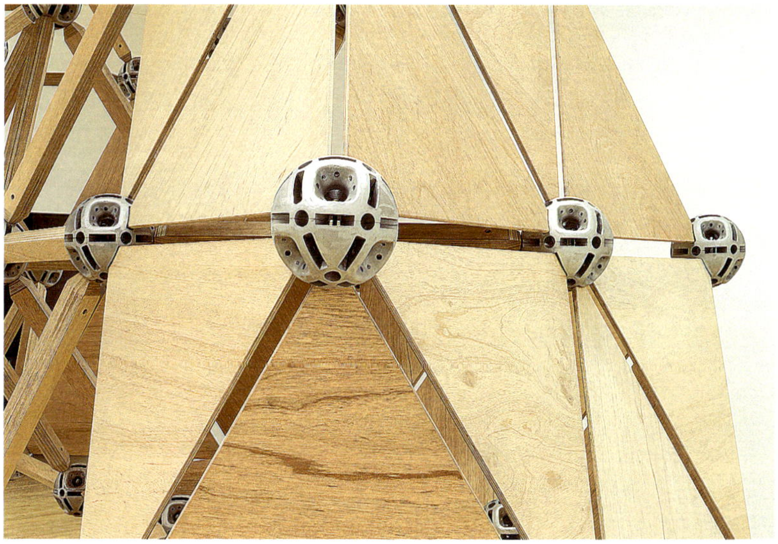

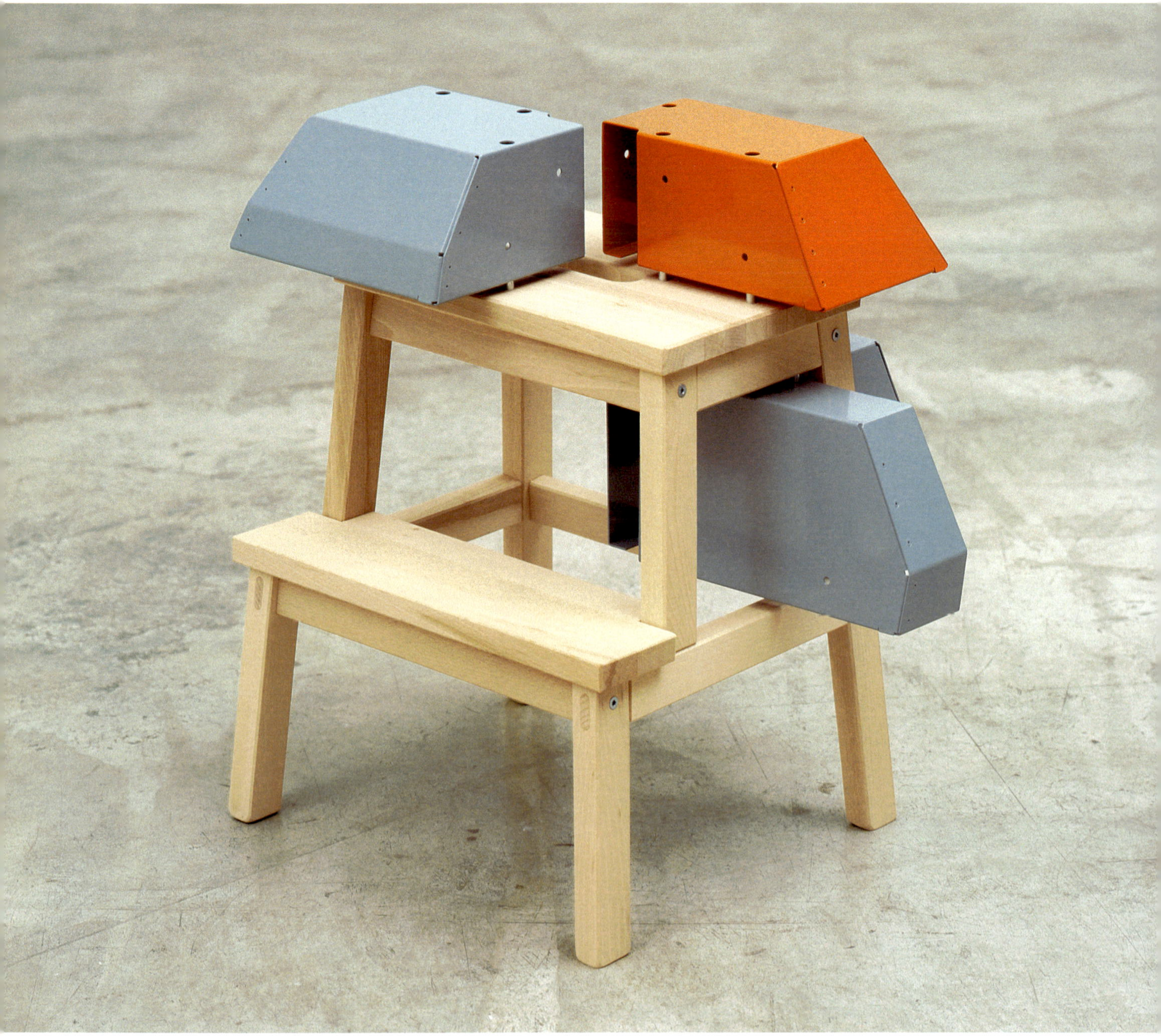

*Andersson*, 2010
Powder coated aluminum enclosures,
IKEA and fasteners
61 x 56 x 56 cm, series of 13

**Following**

*Andersson*, 2010

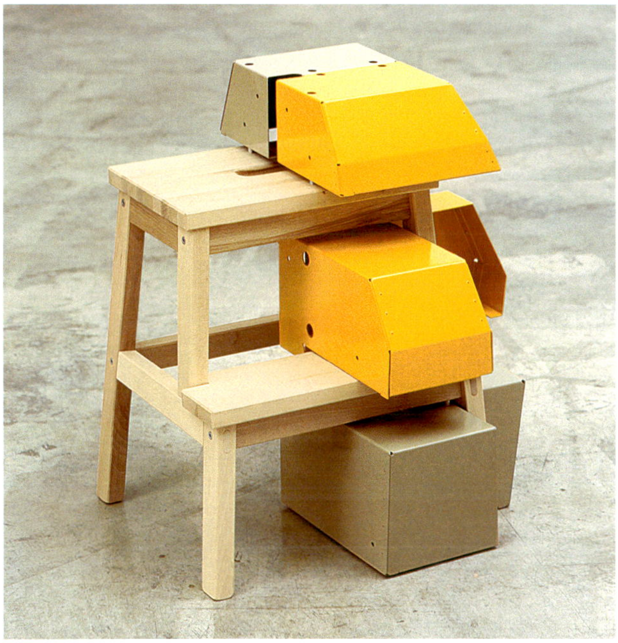
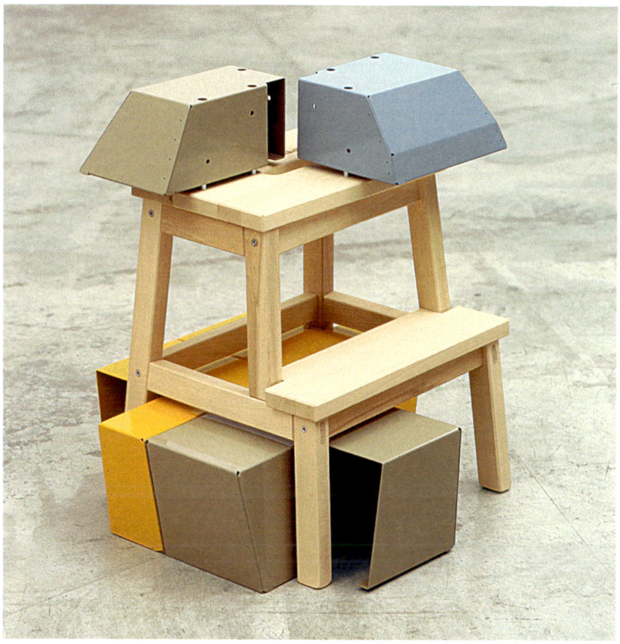
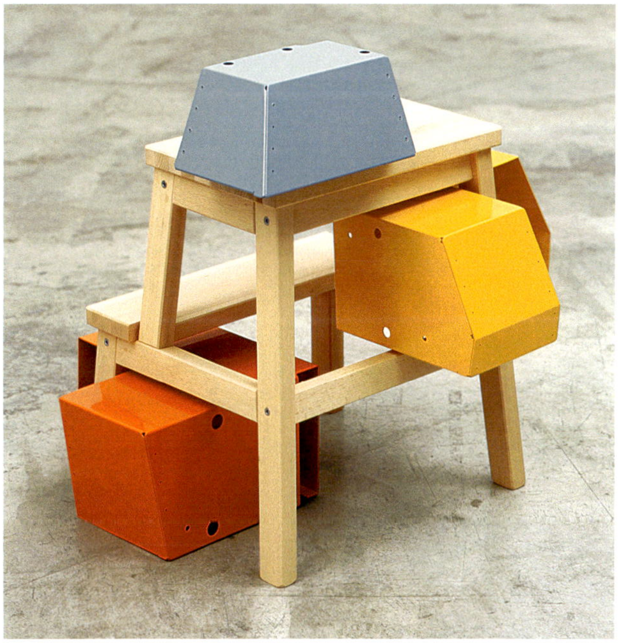
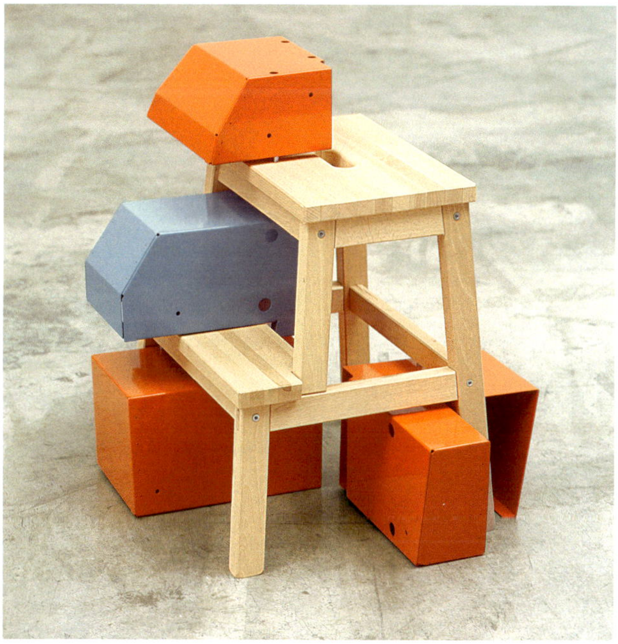

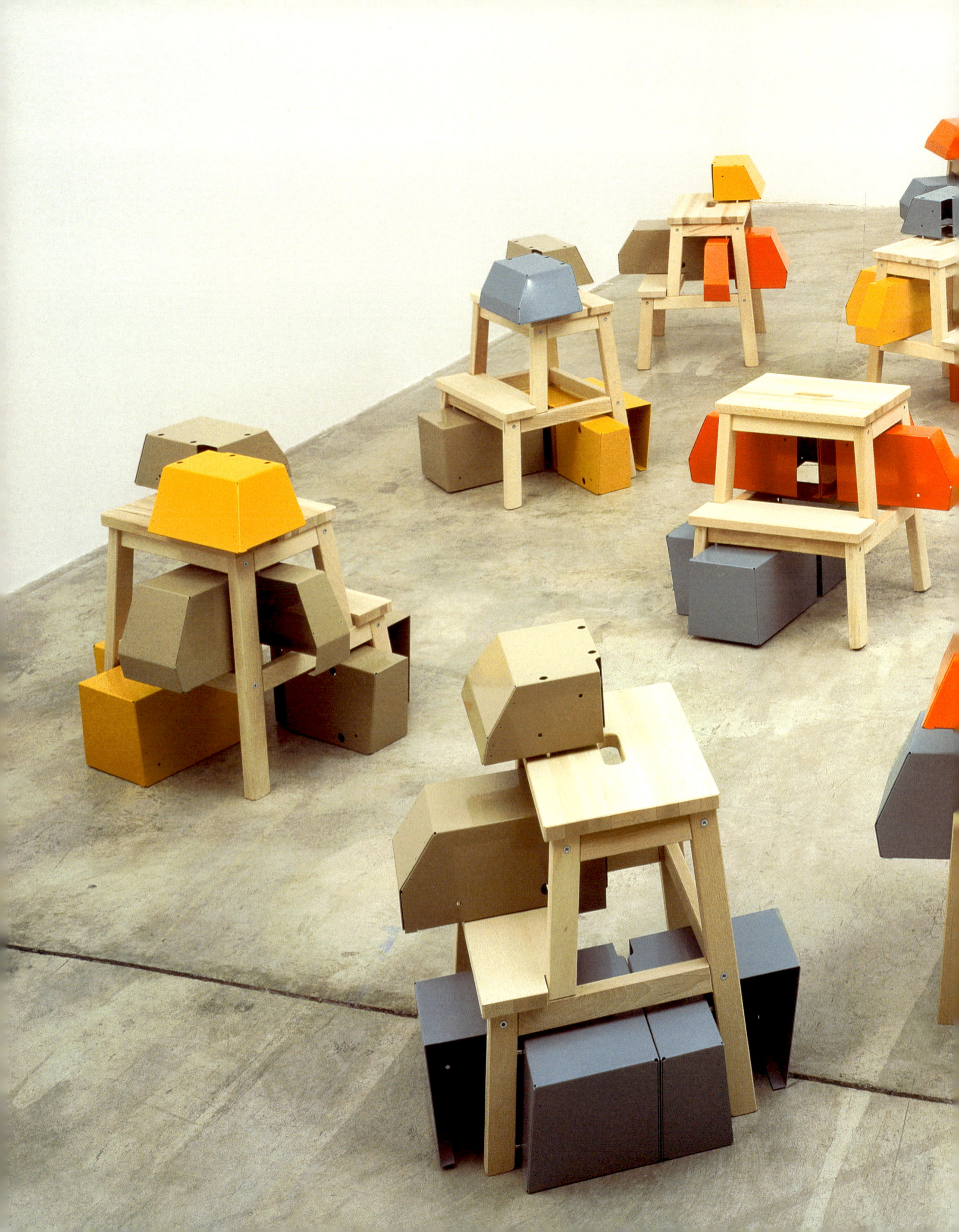

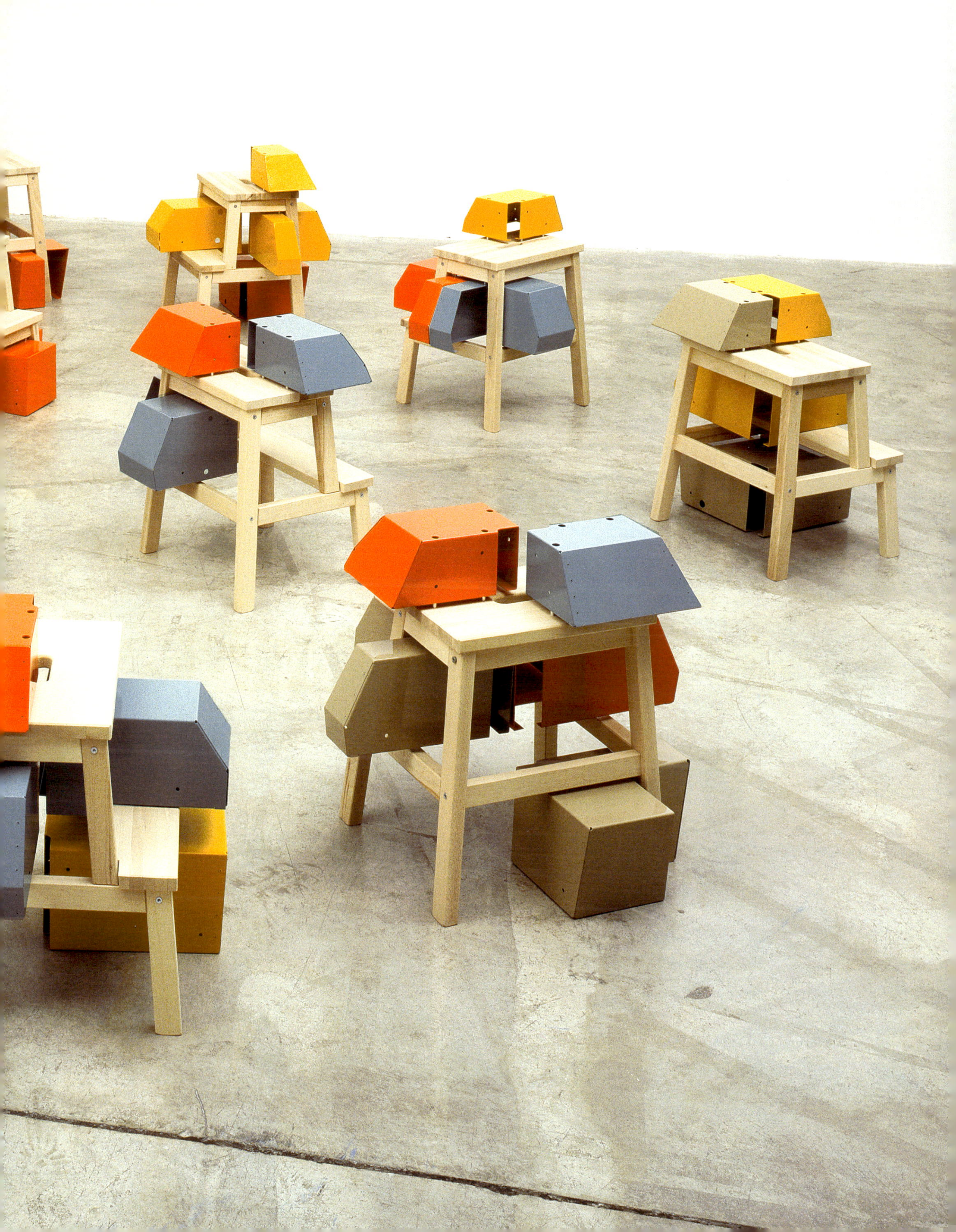

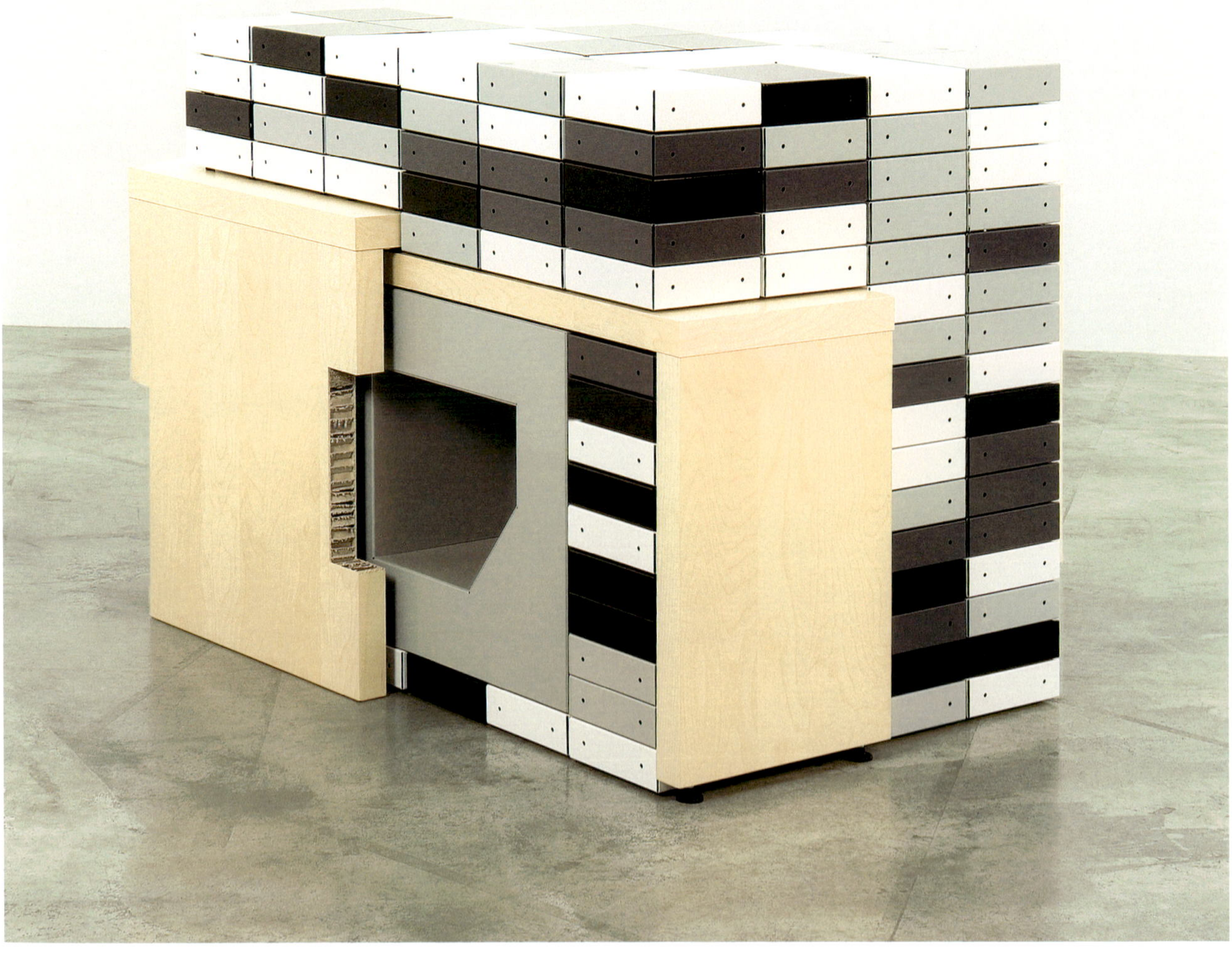

*Jjimjilbang*, 2010
Powder coated aluminum enclosures,
milled IKEA and rubber bumpers
152 x 132 x 94 cm

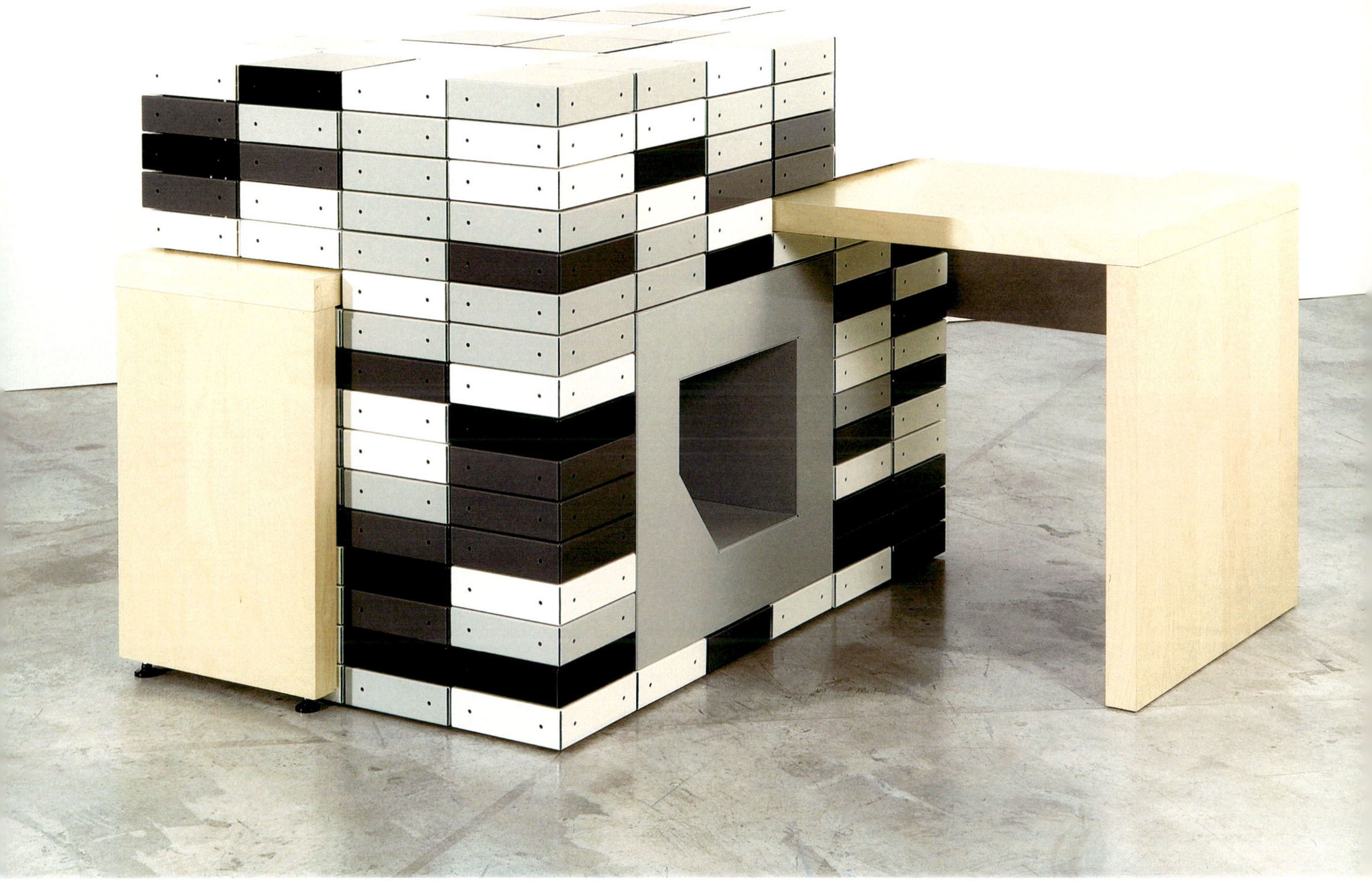

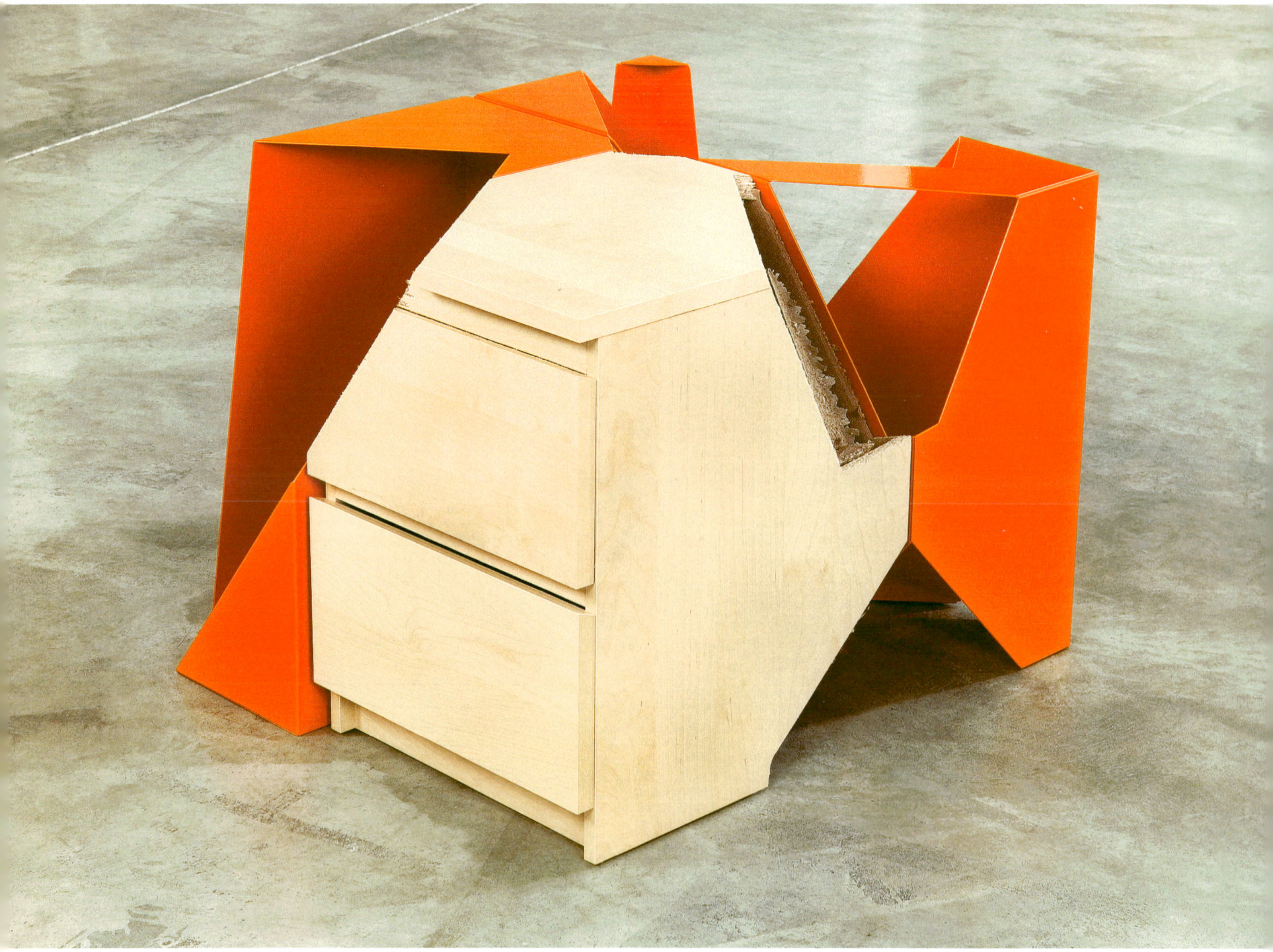

*The Terrorizers* , 2010
Powder coated aluminum enclosures
and milled IKEA
79 x 66 x 56 cm

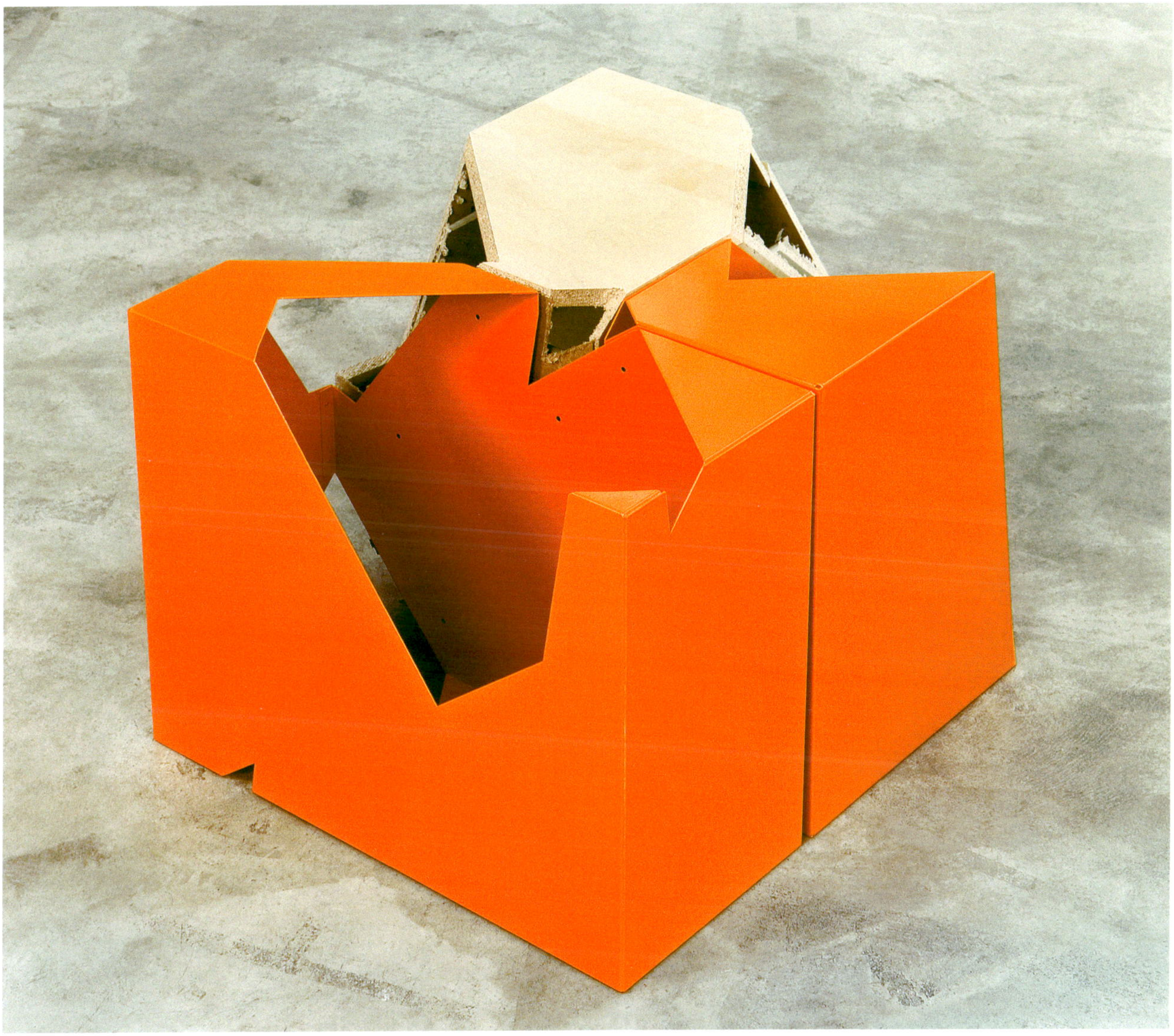

# LIST OF WORKS

*Fullerene*, 2003
Extruded aluminum, synthetic rubber tire, aluminum plate and fasteners
244 cm in diameter

*Access*, 2004
Galvanized steel ductwork
183 x 183 x 183 cm

*Excel*, 2004
Fluorescent light fixtures and steel struts
122 x 122 x 132 cm

*Hayes House (Landscape Proposal for a Public Park)*, 2005
Maquette
50 x 76 x 45 cm

*Alouette*, 2006
Powder coated aluminum, machined PVC and fasteners
74 x 81 cm in diameter

*Cosmos*, 2006
Sheet metal, automotive paint, formed stainless steel tube and fasteners
244 x 152 cm in diameter

*IDCSP*, 2006
Aluminum tube and plate, PVC, vacuum-formed plastic and fasteners
396 x 244 cm in diameter

*IBM 360/85 (Landscape Proposal)*, 2006
Maquette
56 x 81 x 36 cm

*Proposal A*, 2007
Powder coated steel
Digital rendering

*Arthur*, 2008
Powder coated aluminum enclosures, IKEA and rubber bumpers
96 x 102 x 72 cm

*Umbria*, 2008
Powder coated aluminum enclosure, milled IKEA and rubber bumpers
145 x 74 x 74 cm

*Sienna*, 2008
Powder coated aluminum enclosure, milled IKEA and rubber bumpers
145 x 74 x 74 cm

*Mao*, 2008
Powder coated aluminum enclosure, IKEA and rubber bumpers
80 x 80 x 80 cm

*Kermit*, 2008
Powder coated aluminum enclosures, milled IKEA and rubber bumpers
55 x 55 x 82 cm
*Collection of David and Yvonne Fleck*

*Bonsai*, 2008
Powder coated aluminum enclosures, milled IKEA and rubber bumpers
94 x 175 x 132 cm

*Every Building, or Site, that a Building Permit was Issued for a New Building in Toronto in 2006*, 2008
35mm colour motion picture film (1:1.85), no sound, 13 min looping film installation

*Reticulated Gambol*, 2007-08
Powder coated steel
1219 x 1280 x 457 cm
*Commissioned by the City of Toronto under the Art and Landscape collaboration program*

*IBM 360 Panel 40*, 2009
Milled and folded aluminum and custom wall mounts
71 x 69 x 20 cm

*IBM 360 Panel 65*, 2009
Milled and folded aluminum and custom wall mounts
74 x 92 x 22 cm

*50 Light Fixtures from Home Depot*, 2009
35mm colour motion picture film (1:1.33), no sound, 9 min looping film installation
304 x 243 cm fixed projection size

*Andersson*, 2010
Powder coated aluminum enclosures, IKEA and fasteners
61 x 56 x 56 cm, series of 13

*The Terrorizers*, 2010
Powder coated aluminum enclosures and milled IKEA
79 x 66 x 56 cm

*Jjimjilbang*, 2010
Powder coated aluminum enclosures, milled IKEA and rubber bumpers
152 x 132 x 94 cm

*Brave New Waves*, 2010
Powder coated aluminum enclosures, milled IKEA and rubber bumpers
185 x 185 x 41 cm

*Camera Tracking a Spiral Drawn Between the Two Curved Towers of Vijo Revell's Toronto City Hall*, 2010
35mm colour motion picture film (1:1.85), no sound, 9 min looping film installation. Technical collaborator: Mike Sharpe Studios.
*Commissioned by the City of Toronto and Sarah Robayo Sheridan*

*Mr. Smith*, 2011
Cast and machined aluminum, plywood and fasteners
Dimensions variable

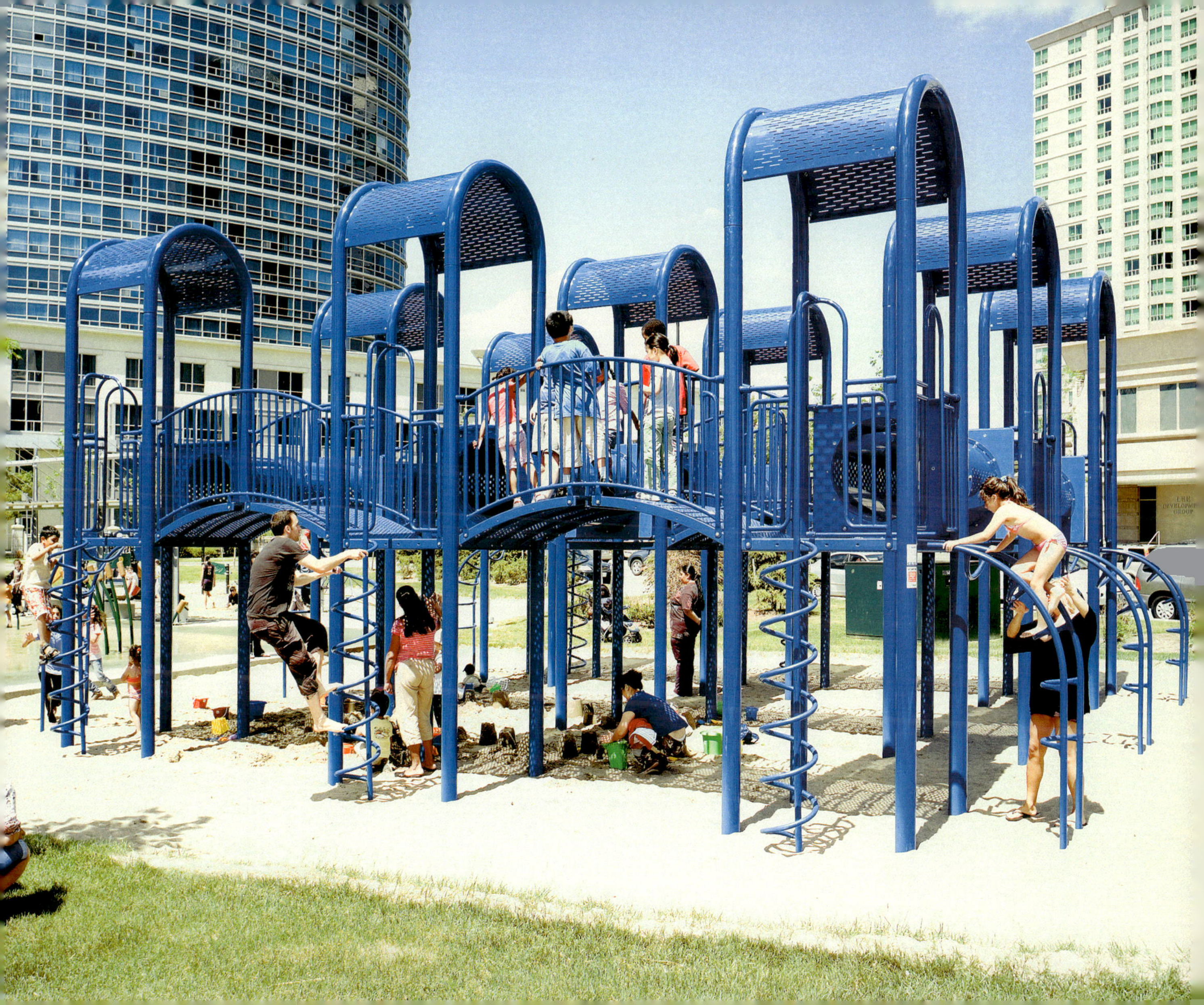

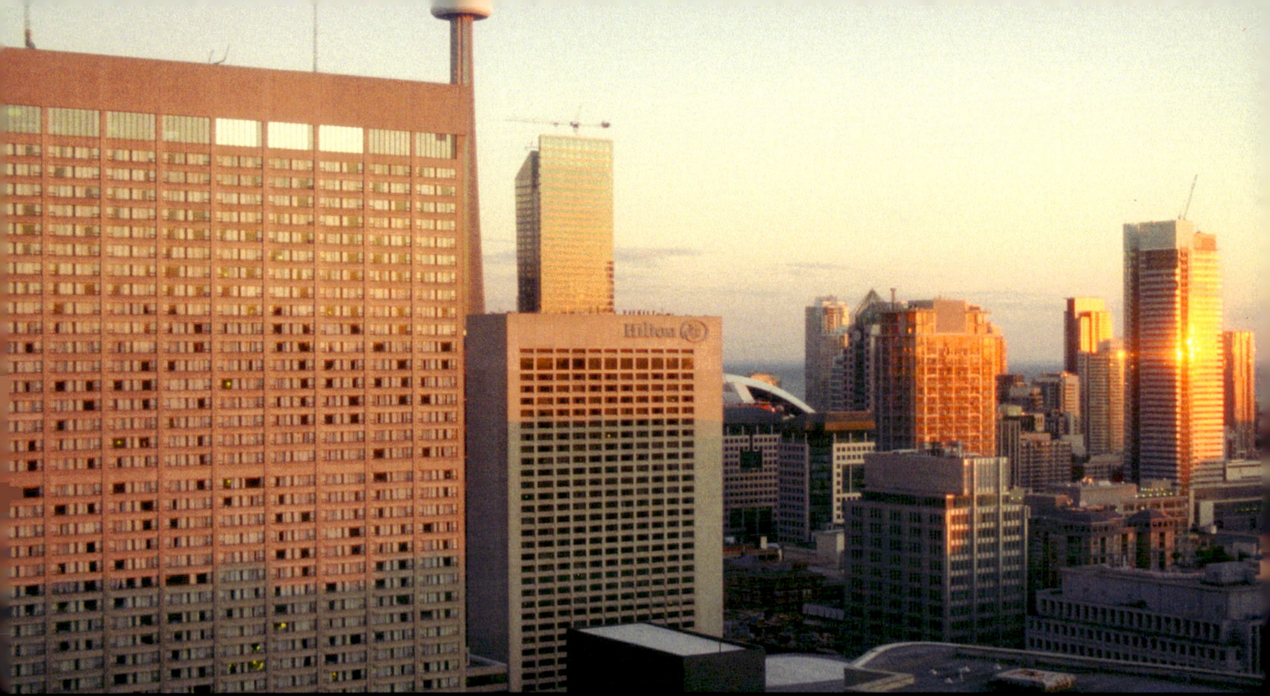
Hilton

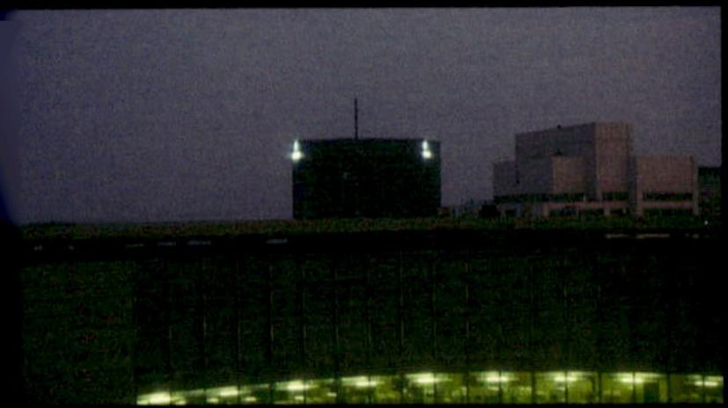

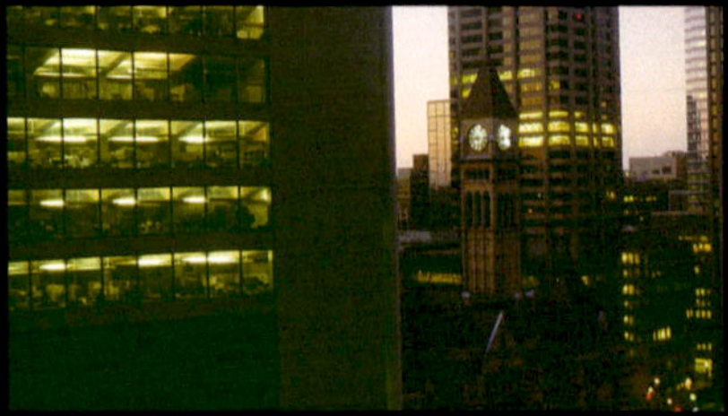

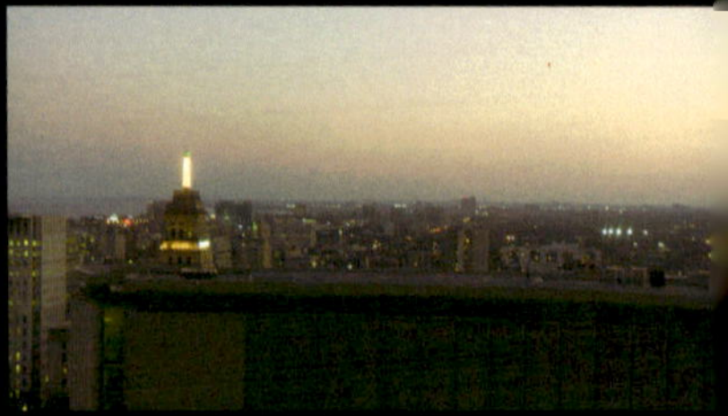

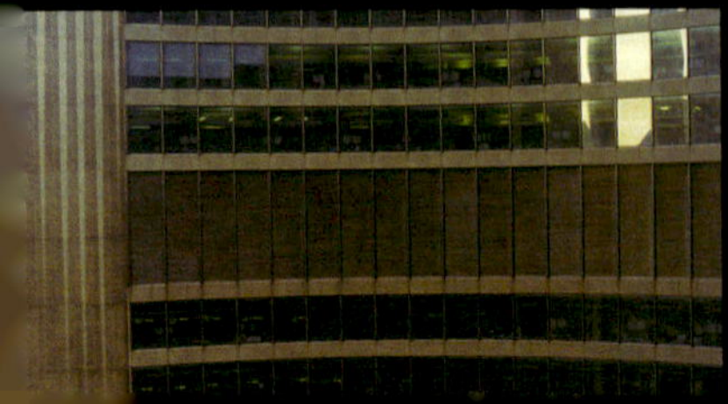

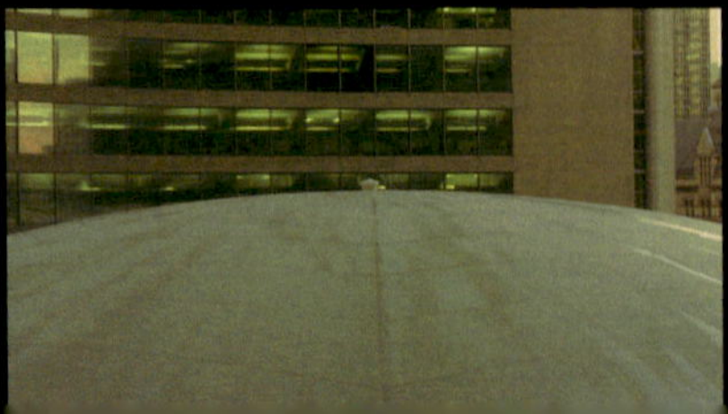

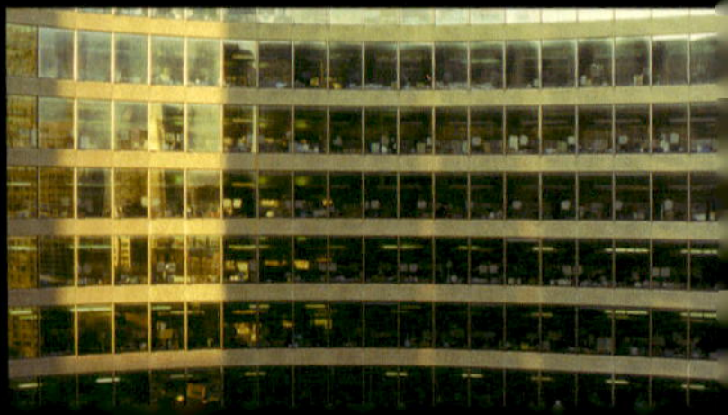

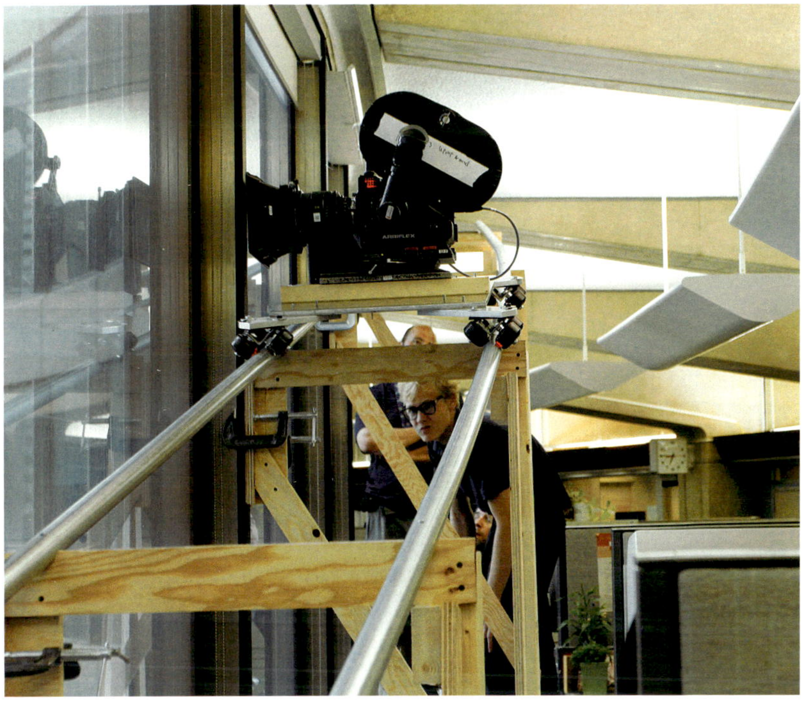

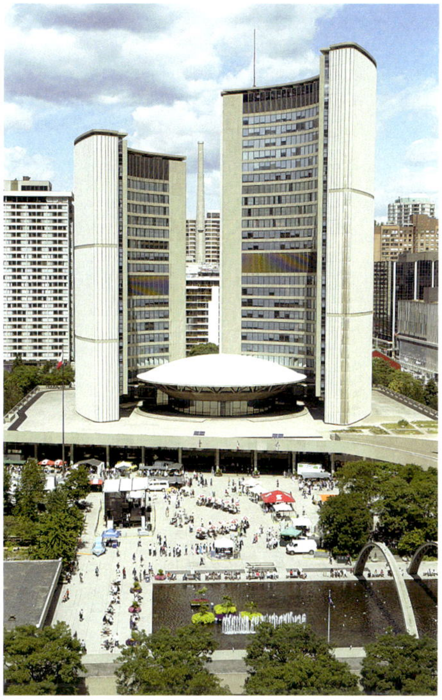

This 35-mm film installation explores the two parabolic towers of Toronto's iconic City Hall. Designed by Finnish architect Viljo Revell and opened in 1965, the architecture stands out for its mid-century futuristic vision. Its two curved towers shape and define an internal volume: the white dome of council chambers. Using the windows that line the two arched towers as framing devices, the moving camera traces a spiralling arc through the building's skeleton, using the architecture itself as the mechanism to generate the work. The spiral begins at the bottom corner of the east tower, making almost two complete revolutions, in twelve tracking shots, as it ascends to the uppermost corner of the west tower. Shot during the magic hours of morning and early evening to catch shifting conditions of light, the looping film is comprised of three complete spirals that reveal the building's interior dialog and the complex relationship it has to its immediate context in Toronto's downtown core.

*Camera Tracking a Spiral...* 2010 (production shot)

Toronto City Hall
*Courtesy of the City of Toronto*

# CURRICULUM VITAE

## Solo Exhibitions

| | |
|---|---|
| 2011 | *Young & Giroux*, Musée d'art contemporain de Montréal, Montréal |
| 2010 | *Beta Boole*, Southern Alberta Art Gallery, Lethbridge |
| | *Beta Boole*, Diaz Contemporary, Toronto |
| | *50 Light Fixtures from Home Depot*, Mercer Union, Toronto |
| 2009 | *Every Building in Toronto*, Prefix ICA, Toronto |
| 2008 | *Boole*, Diaz Contemporary, Toronto |
| 2006 | *Access & Excel*, YYZ Artists' Outlet, Toronto |
| | *Cosmos, Alouette & IDCSP*, Diaz Contemporary, Toronto |
| 2004 | *3 Objects*, Ace Art Inc., Winnipeg |

## Group Exhibitions

| | |
|---|---|
| 2011 | *2011 Sobey Art Award*, Art Gallery of Halifax, Halifax |
| | *Sobey Art Award: 2011 Ontario Long List*, Oakville Galleries, Oakville |
| 2010 | *Everything Must Go*, Art Toronto, Toronto |
| | *The Night of Future Past*, Nuit Blanche, Toronto |
| | *Beyond/In Western New York*, Hallswalls Contemporary Arts Center, Buffalo |
| | EXiS Festival, Seoul |
| | *Traces the Sand Left in the Machine*, Forum Expanded, Berlinale, Berlin |
| | *Kollaps*, Kunstverein Bochum Kulturrat, Bochum |
| 2009 | *Fenomen IKEA*, Museum für Kunst und Gewerbe Hamburg, Hamburg |
| | *Cinema and Disjunction*, EXiS Festival, Seoul (film screening) |
| | *Macht*, Gallery Schafschetzy, Graz, Austria |
| | *Kollaps*, Kunstverein Mistelbach, Mistelbach |
| | *Ontario Sobey Finalists*, Cambridge Galleries, Cambridge |
| | *Cinema and Disjunction*, Pacific Cinematheque, Vancouver (film screening) |
| | *Cinema and Disjunction*, Metro Cinema, Edmonton (film screening) |
| 2008 | *Green House*, Art Gallery of Ontario Rental and Sales Gallery, Toronto |
| | *Cinema and Disjunction*, Cinematheque Ontario, Toronto (film screening) |
| 2007 | MACO: Mexico Arte Contemporaneo, Mexico City |
| | *Group Sculpture Exhibition*, Diaz Contemporary, Toronto |
| 2006 | *We Can Do This Now*, Power Plant Contemporary Art Gallery, Toronto |
| 2005 | *Inaugural Group Show*, Diaz Contemporary, Toronto |
| 2004 | *Public Arts Projects Interactive*, Scope Miami Art Fair, Miami |
| | *The News at Five: Sculpture*, Toronto International Art Fair, Toronto |
| | *Come Up To My Room*, Gladstone Hotel, Toronto |
| 2003 | *Prefabricating Postproduction*, Virus Arts, Toronto |

## Commissioned Projects

| | |
|---|---|
| 2011/12 | *Mt. Dennis Public Art Project*, City of Toronto, Toronto |
| 2011 | *Interregnum: Corner Displacement for John Andrews*, University of Toronto at Scarborough, Toronto |
| 2010/12 | *Canadian Infrastructure Project*, Oakville Galleries, Oakville |
| 2010 | *Camera Tracking a Spiral...*, Nuit Blanche, City of Toronto, Toronto |
| 2007/08 | *Reticulated Gambol*, Lee Centre Park, City of Toronto, Toronto |

## Awards

| | |
|---|---|
| 2011 | Sobey Art Award, short list (5 artists) |
| 2010 | Artist Prize Finalist, Toronto Friends of the Visual Arts |
| 2009 | Sobey Art Award, long list (25 artists) |

### Reviews and Publications

2011 John Pohl, "Playing with sound, silence and the senses," *The Montréal Gazette*, February 12

2010 Faye Hirsch, "Beyond/In Western New York 2010: Alternating...," *Art in America*, December

John Massier, "Beyond/In Western New York 2010: Alternating Currents" *Beyond/In Western New York* (exhibition catalogue)

Ivan Jurakic, "Christian Giroux and Daniel Young," *Border Crossings*, May, No. 114

Gary Michael Dault, "IKEA,cubed and shot through with brightness," *The Globe and Mail*, April 17

Scott Sorli, "Daniel Young and Christian Giroux: Every Building...," *C Magazine*, Spring Issue #105

Forum Expanded, Berlinale 2010 (program catalogue)

"Editors' Picks: 50 Light Fixtures from Home Depot," *Magenta Magazine online*, Winter

Murray Whyte, "Home Depot Lighting as Artistic Fixtures," *The Toronto Star*, January 25

Ian Balfour, "50 Light Fixtures from Home Depot," Mercer Union (exhibition essay)

2009 Jeanette Hepp, "Decorate or Deliberate?," *Sleek Magazine*, Autumn, No.23

Robert Klanten, Sven Ehmann, Andrej Kupetz & Shonquis Moreno (ed.) *Once Upon a Chair*, (Berlin: Gestalten)

Peggy Gale, "Assembling the Givens," EXiS Festival (program catalogue)

Peggy Gale, "Assembling the Givens," *Prefix Photo*, Spring #19

Dan Rubenstein, "Play it Cool," *Surface Magazine*, May/June, Issue 77

Ben Donoghue, "Cinema and Disjunction," Pacific Cinematheque/VIVO (program essay)

Murray Whyte, "Is Toronto A City Built to Last?," *The Toronto Star*, May 7

Dave LeBlanc, "At Play with a Playground," *The Globe and Mail*, April 3

"Material Boys," *indesignlive.com*, March 9

"Best of Toronto: Artists," *NOW Magazine*, October 29 - November 4

2008 Ben Portis, "Tag Team: The Sculptural Conspiracy...," *Canadian Art*, Fall, Vol.25, No.3

Andrea Carson, "Gym Boys," *DesignLines Magazine*, Fall, Vol.7, No.2

Gary Michael Dault, "Christian Giroux and Daniel Young...," *The Globe and Mail*, June 28

Andrea Carson, "Sculpture: Christian Giroux and Daniel Young," *viewoncanadianart.com*, October 16

2007 Jennifer Allen, "Critics Pick: We Can Do This Now," *artforum.com*, January

Ian Carr-Harris, "Toronto," *Contemporary*, June, No.82

2006 Peter Goddard, "Winter Program Takes Flight...," *The Toronto Star*, December 21

Kenneth Hayes, "New Products of the Sheltered Workshop," *Paperwait*, Vol.7

Gary Michael Dault, "Space-age Dreams come to earth," *The Globe and Mail*, May 13

Sarah Robayo Sheridan, "Satellites that Fell to Earth," YYZ Artists' Outlet (exhibition essay)

2005 Camilla Singh, "Constructive Folly," *Canadian Art*, Winter, Vol.22, No.1

Mary Reid, "3 Objects," *C Magazine*, Spring, Issue #85

2004 Daniel Chang, "Notebook," *Miami Herald*, December 3

Kenneth Hayes, "New Products of the Sheltered Workshop," Aceartinc. (exhibition essay)

Thomas Hirshmann, "Get a Room," *NOW Magazine*, February 12 - 18

2003 Ben Portis, "Prefabricating Postproduction," *Canadian Art*, Fall, Vol.20, No.4

Thomas Hirshmann, "Hot Young Blood," *NOW Magazine*, July 3 - 10

Sarah Milroy, "Critic's Choice," *The Globe and Mail*, July 19

Betty Ann Jordan, "Prefabricating Postproduction," *Toronto Life*, June 30

### Residencies

2011/12 Canada Council for the Arts, International Studio Program: Berlin

2009 York University Digital Sculpture Lab, Toronto

2006 Canada Council for the Arts, International Studio Program: Paris

### Curatorial Projects

2004 *Constructive Folly*, Doris McCarthy Gallery, Scarborough, ON

## ACKNOWLEDGEMENTS

We would like to thank our curator Ryan Doherty, who made this catalogue possible and the staff at the SAAG for their invaluable help bringing this project to fruition. We are indebted to Ken, Jesse and Mark for their formidable essays and to Lisa for her excellent design work.

We wish to extend our gratitude to the tremendous network of architects, engineers, designers, digital animators, projector technicians, machinists, carpenters, fabricators, suppliers and contractors of all kinds with whom we have consulted, contracted, haggled, befriended and learned from over the past nine years, and without whom none of this would have been possible.

Warm thanks to Benjamin Diaz and the past and present staff at Diaz Contemporary for their ongoing support.

And lastly, we would like to thank our community of mentors, colleagues and friends that hold us accountable and challenge us daily. Without their support, Dan would have gone into the renewable energy sector a long time ago.